THE RADICAL LEFT AND
AMERICAN FOREIGN POLICY

Studies in International Affairs Number 15

P12

Studies in International Affairs Number 15

THE RADICAL LEFT AND AMERICAN FOREIGN POLICY

Robert W. Tucker

The Washington Center of Foreign Policy Research
School of Advanced International Studies
The Johns Hopkins University

The Johns Hopkins Press, Baltimore and London

The Johns Hopkins Press, Baltimore, Maryland 21218
The Johns Hopkins Press Ltd., London

ISBN 0-8018-1224-0 (cloth)
ISBN 0-8018-1225-9 (paper)

Originally published, 1971
Paperbound edition, 1971
Second printing (cloth and paper), 1972
Third printing (paper), 1973

FOREWORD

Historical revisionism—the reinterpretation of events to refute the conventional view of the past—is a recurrent phenomenon in America, particularly in the aftermath of unpopular wars. Revisionism serves several functions. It may reveal reality in a new light; it may exhibit an important strand of thinking in the intellectual foundations of public policy; or it may create historical "myths" that influence opinion and policy.

The passage of time and events following America's painful intervention in the Vietnamese war has not yet disclosed what influence the historiography of the radical left will exert on policy, although it has certainly influenced the opinion of students. It is not too early, however, to examine this latest recurrence of postwar revisionism as a reconstruction of reality and a symptom of the changing American approach to the outside world. In both respects historians of the radical left—whatever one may think of the professional merits of their work—provide important insights into the momentous drama of the expansion of American power, commitments, and interests since World War II. In both respects they provoke us to consider in a new light the future course of the American "empire."

Professor Robert W. Tucker's essay examines the revisionism of the radical left as a profound student of the American approach to foreign policy. Like his previous booklet in this series, *Nation or Empire? The Debate Over American Foreign Policy*, and its companion, Professor Liska's *War and Order: Reflections on Vietnam and History*, this study views the present transitional stage of American foreign policy in an analytical perspective transcending the current events and opinions that preoccupy our attention. Like the recent quadrennial volume *America and the World*, published by the Washington Center of Foreign Policy Research in 1970, this booklet is part of the Center's continuing project, supported by the Ford Foundation, to monitor and assess major trends in American foreign policy.

ROBERT E. OSGOOD
Director
Washington Center of
Foreign Policy Research

ACKNOWLEDGMENTS

This essay grew out of a graduate seminar on the radical left and American foreign policy. I am indebted to the members of the seminar and above all to those who refused to be deterred from sharp criticism of my views of American diplomacy. One member of the seminar, Patrick Magrath, ably assisted me throughout and his considerable efforts deserve special mention.

Among colleagues and friends who read the essay in various forms and gave me the benefit of their advice and criticism, I am particularly grateful to George Liska, Roger Hansen, Piero Gleijeses, and Robert E. Osgood.

CONTENTS

I. Introduction   1

II. Conventional and Radical Critiques of American Foreign Policy   21

III. The Radical Critique Assessed   55

IV. A Concluding Note   146

THE RADICAL LEFT AND
AMERICAN FOREIGN POLICY

I. INTRODUCTION

It is by now a commonplace that the war in Vietnam led to a breakdown in the foreign policy consensus of the past generation. But commonplaces can be misleading. The lasting effects of the debate occasioned by Vietnam remain far from apparent. Even the significance of the debate itself remains unclear once the radical critique of the war, and of American policy generally, is excluded.

Thus it is unclear whether the majority of conventional—that is, liberal and moderate—critics of the war came to oppose the conflict because they concluded it could not have a successful outcome, or because they concluded that whatever the outcome the costs had become disproportionate to the interests at stake, or, finally, because they did not share the outlook and interests that were bound, sooner or later, to lead to a Vietnam. In the light of the history of the war, however, and of the correlation between its costly yet frustrating course and the swelling ranks of critics, the only reasonable conclusion is that most conventional critics based their opposition primarily upon the first and second of these grounds rather than the third. It does not necessarily follow, as some radical critics insist, that liberal opposition to the war has been based throughout upon mere expediency, that it has been a pragmatic opposition not a principled one. It does follow that the opposition to the war, insofar as it has been based upon considerations of cost and effectiveness, leaves essentially intact the broad consensus the war is commonly alleged to have ruptured.

To the extent the debate has transcended Vietnam and dealt with American policy generally—that is, with America's role and interests in the world at large—its significance appears still less apparent. It is of course clear that conventional critics of the war are opposed to intervening in the kind of conflict America has encountered in Vietnam. But this opposition can scarcely be equated with anti-interventionism, *per se*, whether in Asia or elsewhere. It cannot be and has not been equated with an anti-interventionist policy where intervention is undertaken in response to overt aggression by a Communist power against a nation allied to America or against a nation, allied or not, whose survival is considered important to American security. It cannot be equated even with an anti-interventionist policy where intervention takes the form of direct military involvement in what is predominantly an internal revolutionary conflict. (In this hemisphere, it remains uncertain whether one law of American policy, that there must be "no second Cuba," has been repealed.)

To be sure, it is generally agreed that in the future America should not resort to military intervention where a government, though provided with forms of assistance other than military forces, cannot fend for itself against insurrectionary elements (if it can do so there is no need to intervene with military forces). But to this proscription is commonly attached the qualification that the nation or region in question not constitute, in itself, a vital strategic interest, or that, quite apart from the intrinsic importance of the immediate area of conflict, the outcome of the conflict not prove generally destabilizing. If the first of these

qualifications leaves ample room for dispute and uncertainty, it does at least suggest a test, however obvious, that in principle may be applied prior to the
act of intervention. At best, however, the application
of the second qualification is bound to prove highly
speculative until such time as the consequences intervention is designed to prevent are already apparent.

It is easy enough to point to the difficulties attending attempts to lay down rules for determining when
to intervene and when not to intervene which are
neither so general that they are largely irrelevant nor
so qualified that their application depends almost entirely upon the particular circumstances attending intervention. These difficulties may be resolved only by
the decision to exclude the possibility of intervention
in certain well defined areas, whatever the consequences of inactivity. It is significant, though hardly
surprising, that very few conventional critics have
seen fit to indicate such areas (Africa, perhaps,
apart). Thus the broader consequences of the debate
engendered by Vietnam remain obscure if only for
the reason that most of the articulate and influential
opponents of the war continue to support one of the
principal foundations on which America's Asian policy has long rested—the need to maintain a balance
of power in Asia. The maintenance of an Asian balance of power presumably requires, in turn, the containment of Chinese power. The debate over America's Asian policy has therefore turned largely
around the issue of the nature of the Chinese threat
and the appropriate means for countering this threat,
but not whether the threat should be countered.
While many opponents of the war in Vietnam have
insistently discounted the prospect of direct Chinese
expansion through conventional military methods,

3

they have not opposed meeting such expansion, should it ever occur, with American military power. Even so austere and unconventional a critic of America's Asian policy as Walter Lippmann, though opposing in any circumstances the commitment of American forces to a large land war on the Asian mainland, has never opposed the use of other forms of American military power, if necessary, to contain direct Chinese expansion.

Given these considerations, the rather muted response to the Nixon Doctrine by liberal and moderate critics of American foreign policy is understandable. For the Nixon Doctrine, particularly in its application to Asia, holds out the promise of no more Vietnams, though not at the price of sacrificing what continue to be regarded as America's vital interests—above all, the containment of China. In a more general sense, the Nixon Doctrine is evidently intended to answer the charge of American "globalism" by disavowing a policy of unlimited and indiscriminate commitment to the end of preventing Communist expansion. The central thesis of that doctrine is that the United States "will participate in the defense and development of allies and friends, but that America cannot—and will not—conceive *all* the plans, design *all* the programs, execute all the decisions and undertake *all* the defense of the free nations of the world." As a statement of intent, the Nixon Doctrine is hardly a striking response to the critics of American globalism. Whether it will satisfy these critics will evidently depend upon the meaning eventually given the Nixon Doctrine in practice. It is worth recalling, however, that from Truman to Nixon each administration has looked to Asian states to assume primary responsibility for their defense

4

against non-nuclear aggression, and particularly to assume primary responsibility for defending themselves against internal subversion.

But even if it is assumed that despite its cautious and rather banal formulation the Nixon Doctrine represents a triumph of sorts for the so-called limitationist critique, the consequences of the triumph for policy are by no means apparent. What, after all, is the meaning of limitationism other than what the term itself implies: that there are limits to a nation's, any nation's, power and that these limits must in turn set limits to a nation's interests and purposes. The principle is unexceptionable as a counsel of prudence and as a warning against the hubris to which the powerful of the world have regularly succumbed. At the same time, it need not prove incompatible with an expansionist and imperial outlook. It is only incompatible with an unlimited expansionist and imperial outlook. Not infrequently, it has been interpreted to mean that domestic policy and needs should have primacy over foreign policy, save when the nation's vital interests are at stake. This meaning is not inherent in the principle. Even if it were, it would only succeed in raising the issues of what comprises the nation's vital interests and what constitutes a threat to those interests. There are no persuasive grounds for asserting that in America's case the answers to these issues are somehow apparent once the primacy of domestic policy is acknowledged.

Moreover, to the extent the new orthodoxy of the Nixon Doctrine accepts the conventional criticism of yesterday, it does so largely in the sense that it accepts the conventionally critical view of the threat held out to American interests. This view, with its emphasis on a world that is politically and ideologically pluralistic, did not call for an essential change in the definition of American interests. To the contrary, the principal thrust of the conventional critique was precisely that, given the proper response, the contemporary world does not hold out a serious threat to those interests. A pluralistic world, though far more complicated than the world of a generation ago, is nevertheless a safer world. Interpreted, in essence, as the triumph of nationalism, pluralism not only means that Communist expansion no longer carries the threat to America it once carried, it also means that the prospect of Communist expansion has dramatically declined. The consequence of pluralism, it is concluded, is, if not a marked decline in the need for order, then at least a marked decline in the need for intervention—certainly military intervention—as a means for preserving an order compatible with American interests. Provided only that its optimistic assumptions are correct, the reasons for the triumph of this critique in the aftermath of Vietnam need not be labored.

In retrospect, it is difficult to escape the conclusion that what is perhaps most striking about the debate occasioned by Vietnam is the extent to which ostensible adversaries shared the same basic conceptions of America's role and interests in the world. If Vietnam revealed the changes that have occurred over two decades in the structure of American security, if the war and the ensuing debate have shown that many of America's present interests and commitments can no longer be justified by a conception of security that could once plausibly account for these same interests and commitments, there has nevertheless been little indication of a disposition among conventional critics to draw the consequences. The principal reason for this disinclination is that most critics share substantially the same views of America's position in the world as do the avowed supporters of American policy. For both, America has a vital interest in maintaining a certain kind of world order—one in which America will not only continue to occupy a preponderant position in the international hierarchy but a world in which change may be effected only in certain ways and certain types of change may be precluded altogether.

* * *

These considerations lend support to the radical left's view that the debate occasioned by Vietnam has been largely an in-house debate, that the core of the debate has concerned the problem of means rather than the critical issue of interests, and that, in consequence, the significance of the debate—the radical critique apart—is that it has no real significance, confined as it has been to the question of how the American empire should be administered but not whether there should be an American empire. If there is much to be said for this view, it is nonetheless overdrawn. Above all, it too airily dismisses the problem of means. To say that the core of the debate has concerned the problem of means is not to dismiss the importance of the problem. It may well be that the nature of American interests must broadly account for the methods of American policy and that the latter cannot be altered without altering the former. The point remains that interests may be altered, if not abandoned altogether, by the refusal to employ certain means in their pursuit. It seems clear that the abandonment of an overtly interventionist policy, particularly in Asia, would eventually result in the sacrifice of substantial American interests. The interests, as such, might not be foresworn. Moreover, they might still be pursued by any and all means which fall short of military intervention. Still, the refusal to employ, or meaningfully to threaten, force might be expected to alter the nature of American interests. Whether the experience of Vietnam, and the promise of the Nixon Doctrine, will lead to this result remains an open question. Certainly, there is much room for skepticism on this score. But the question cannot be dismissed.

The issue of means apart, it is clear that the radical critique may be distinguished from other criticism by virtue of its rejection of America's role and interests in the world. These interests are seldom, if ever, differentiated. Instead, they are simply characterized as imperialistic, and their condemnation follows. At the same time, the demand that the empire be dismantled—that America abandon its present role and interests—cannot be seen as an end in itself. It is because most radicals find an intimate and even a dependent relationship between American interests abroad and the maintenance of the nation's domestic institutions that they are so insistent upon dismantling the empire. For the empire is at once the outgrowth of those institutions and, increasingly, a condition of their continued maintenance. This being the case, to demand that America abandon its present role and interests is, in effect, to demand that American institutions be radically transformed. Far from being an end in itself, the radical rejection of American foreign policy is primarily intended as a means for the transformation of domestic society. If for no other reason than this, the isolationism of the radical left ought not to be confused with the isolationism of yesterday (or, for that matter, with the neo-isolationism of today), which found in America's involvement abroad a threat to the nation's institutions. In contrast to a traditional isolationism, the isolationism of the radical left must be understood as a provisional isolationism. It is only a Capitalist America that is a repressive force in the world and that must be isolated from the world. With the advent of socialism, however, the reason for isolationism would disappear, for a Socialist America would presumably be a liberating force in the world.

Not only must the isolationism of the radical left be distinguished from the mainstream of American isolationism, the revisionism of the radical left must be distinguished from revisionism generally. Although the radical interpretation of American diplomacy is of necessity revisionist, the converse does not follow. Instead, a revisionist interpretation of American diplomacy may reflect a quite traditional view of statecraft. Certainly, the position that the United States behaved during the immediate post-World War II period in much the same manner great states in comparable situations have behaved in the past is revisionist when placed alongside an orthodox historiography of the cold war. It is no part of an orthodox interpretation to allow that American leaders quite consciously—if not quite consistently—sought to attain a position, with its attendant advantages, which their preponderant power enabled them to attain. Yet this revisionism bears little resemblance to the revisionism of radical historiography. Not only does it differ considerably from the radical version in its reconstruction of the way in which the cold war arose and developed, but this difference reflects a profound disparity of view as to the sources of America's behavior.

Thus the revisionism of radical historiography is distinctive if only by virtue of the consistency with which the American diplomatic record is condemned (though not for its mistakes, as in a conventionally critical historiography, but rather for its successes. In radical historiography, American diplomacy may be considered a crime, but until very recently it is not considered a mistake). In their indictment of what America has done and is doing in the world, radical critics not only depict American behavior in far darker colors than do other critics. In reading them, one is tempted to conclude, despite their protestations to the contrary, that they too share, though in inverted form, the belief in America's exceptionalism. "By any objective standard," one radical critic has written, "the United States has become the most aggressive power in the world, the greatest threat to world peace, to national self-determination, and to international cooperation."[1] To another, unwilling to content himself merely with the present, we are "history's most violent nation."[2] If these are extreme views, even for many radical critics, they are nevertheless suggestive of the unrelentingly harsh judgment radical historiography as a whole passes on American diplomacy in this century. That judgment not only finds America wanting when it is measured by the ideals the nation has professed (something a moderate critic could equally find), it also finds America wanting even when it is measured by rela-

[1] Noam Chomsky, *American Power and the New Mandarins* (1969), pp. 399–400.
[2] Carl Oglesby, "Vietnamese Crucible," in Carl Oglesby and Richard Shaull, *Containment and Change* (1967), p. 42.

tive standards of conduct. It is not so much the moral absolutism that is significant in the radical critique, though this is surely one of its characteristic features, but the judgment, whether explicit or implicit, that American behavior suffers by comparison with the behavior of others. America's prime responsibility for imposing the cold war on a war-torn world is only the most notable example of a theme that runs throughout radical historiography.

Even more than a distinctive account of how aggressively we have behaved as a nation, the radical critique is distinguished from other criticism by its explanation of why we have so behaved. The central theme of radical historiography is of course America's persistent expansionism. That this expansion occurred, if not quite by accident, then without forethought and grand design, is dismissed. There is nothing accidental in America's expansion. Nor is there anything "natural" about it, whether in the sense that it has been inherent in the inordinate growth of American power or in the sense that it has resulted from the dynamics of state competition (a process that presumably gives rise to compulsions which operate independently of the economic and social structures of states). The admission that America's expansion has been, in large measure, simply a function of the growth of American power is as unacceptable to the radical historian as the admission that expansion has been the at least partly unintended result of the search for security. Other nations have had a security problem in this century but not America. And if America does at last have a security problem today, it has been created by our expansion and aggressiveness. If we are at last insecure, though not physically so, we are so insecure precisely for the reason, and to the extent, that our welfare as a nation has been increasingly defined in terms of our imperial position and the inequities on which this position rests.

What does explain America's persistent expansion, in the radical view, is a socio-economic structure. America's interests in the world are the necessary outgrowth of this structure and of the forces it has generated. To the degree there is a consensus on the nature of America's institutions, however repressive the nature of that consensus, there must be a like consensus on the essential interests of America abroad. To the degree that ostensible critics of American foreign policy share in this domestic consensus, they must also be expected to share similar views on the American role in the world. And even in those exceptional instances where critics clearly break from American imperialism, though continuing to share the domestic consensus, the significance of the break must prove limited precisely because the root sources of imperialism are ignored or misread. The essence of the radical critique is not simply that America is aggressive and imperialistic but that it is so out of an institutional necessity. It is the central assumption that American imperialism must ultimately be traced to the institutional structure of American capitalism that is the common denominator of radical criticism. It is the same assumption that most clearly separates radical criticism from all other criticism, whether liberal or moderate left.[3]

[3] An example of what is here termed the moderate left may be found in the volume of essays entitled *A Dissenter's Guide to Foreign Policy* (1968), edited by Irving Howe. Most of the essays were previously published in *Dissent*. In his foreword to the volume Lewis Coser identifies the contributors as belonging

Any attempt to summarize a body of critical thought immediately encounters the objection that it fails to make significant distinctions. It is trite though true to say that if there are similarities there are also important differences among critics of American diplomacy categorized in this essay as radical left. The question is whether these differences overshadow the similarities and, even more, whether the similarities themselves are more apparent than real. Is it even meaningful to speak of a radical left criticism if such criticism is extended to include a William A.

---

to the "radical left" and sharing in common "only the conviction that the old shibboleths and the received wisdom of the left are no longer a sufficient guide, if they ever were, to the unprecedented problems of the New World we now face" (p. 7). Yet it hardly seems appropriate to label as radical left such writers as Michael Harrington, Arnold Kaufman, William Pfaff, Robert Heilbroner, and Irving Howe—to name only some of the contributors—unless the "radical left" is equated with almost any position that is, in Coser's words, "distant, though not equidistant, from the twin pieties of the Cold War stalwarts and certain New Left champions..." (8). But this identification renders the term "radical left" virtually meaningless even in this context. In fact, the contributors range across a very wide spectrum. In their views of foreign policy, if there is anything that holds them together (with, perhaps, the exception of Harrington), it is the belief that the problems of American foreign policy cannot be expected to yield to some simple explanation—and solution. And they cannot be expected to do so because they cannot be reduced to any one root or basic source which, once perceived, may then ultimately be transformed. In a word, if there is a common denominator of these analyses it is precisely the rejection of a radical outlook. Whereas the radical left finds American foreign policy irredeemable so long as American society remains essentially unchanged, the moderate left does not believe that significant change in foreign policy must await a basic transformation of American society. It does not accept the necessity of this parallel because it does not accept the assumption that American foreign policy is simply—or even primarily—the result of forces generated by American capitalism.

13

Williams and a Gabriel Kolko? Whereas Kolko sees American foreign policy as directly responsive to the forces generated by American capitalism, Williams sees this policy as largely responsive to a deeply rooted, though apparently mistaken, conviction about the requirements of the nation's institutions. For Kolko, America's persistent expansion is clearly the result of institutional necessity. Moreover, what American capitalism gave rise to it cannot do without. The empire is necessary to the continued viability of the system as presently constituted. Thus Kolko can find in the liberation of the Third World the key to the liberation of the First. ". . . The rest of the world," Kolko writes, "is forced to do for the American people what they are only tangentially presently able and willing to do for themselves. The victims of American executioners, ironically, thereby work not only for their own integrity and freedom but indirectly for that of the American people themselves."[4] For Williams, what false perceptions gave rise to, the system, even as presently constituted, can do without. Accordingly, the empire is not necessary. Nor is

---

[4] *The Roots of American Foreign Policy* (1969), p. 137. The interaction of the First and Third Worlds is of course a theme of many radical critics. Cf. Herbert Marcuse, *An Essay on Liberation* (1969), pp. 79–85. "[By] virtue of the evolution of imperialism, the developments in the Third World pertain to the dynamic of the First World, and the forces of change in the former are not extraneous to the latter; the 'external proletariat' is a basic factor of potential change within the dominion of corporate capitalism." But if the national liberation fronts have become "an essential part of the opposition within the capitalist metropolis," Marcuse finds that "the exemplary force, the ideological power of the external revolution, can come to fruition only if the structure and cohesion of the capitalist system begin to disintegrate. The chain of exploitation must break at its strongest link."

14

the solution to America's problems to be found abroad. On Williams' view, what Kolko and others have done is what America's leaders have always done. In both, opportunity and difficulty, good and evil, are externalized. The difference is that the latter have defined America's well-being in terms of America's economic and political expansion whereas the former have defined America's well-being in terms of the world's successful resistance to this expansion.

If these differences clearly cannot be ignored, their significance ought not to be exaggerated. Whatever the differences that may separate them, Williams and Kolko substantially agree in their appraisal of the results of American policy. Williams may find the history of American diplomacy tragic because we have denied our better self, whereas Kolko may find no tragedy in this history because we have no better self. Williams may take America's professed ideals seriously, though he believes we have constantly subverted them in practice, whereas Kolko may dismiss these ideals as no more than empty rhetoric. In the end, however, there is no marked disagreement between the two on the way we have behaved in the world or on what we must do in order to redeem ourselves. If Kolko is the economic determinist, par excellence, and Williams the idealist, as so many of his friendly critics have portrayed him, the fact remains that the results of their respective analyses point in the same direction.

Is there an unbridgable difference even with respect to their analyses of the sources of American behavior? One must doubt it. Clearly, Williams places great emphasis on the importance of ideas as an independent force in history. In reading him and those who follow him, it is easy to conclude that the ultimate source of American diplomacy has been a freely floating, though all-determining, conviction that the health of our institutions has necessitated our expansion. But the questions the Williams view must raise are: What has given rise to this conviction and what explains its persistence if, as Williams maintains, it is mistaken? Is not the unavoidable answer that capitalism bred a psychology of expansion and that this psychology struck a particularly deep root in the American character? Is not the answer also that so long as American society is predominantly a Capitalist society the conviction Williams decries will nevertheless persist? Williams' necessity may be a psychic necessity but his psychic necessity is still, at bottom, an institutional necessity.

These issues must be examined at greater length. Here it is sufficient simply to record the assumption that informs this essay. There is a distinctive view of American diplomacy that may be termed radical, despite the many differences which may and do arise among those who share it. In the context of the event that has given the radical critique an appeal it would otherwise never have possessed, these differences have been manifest. Although there is a series of critiques of Vietnam that may be termed radical because they share certain broad assumptions about the nature and causes of the war, there are still diverse radical explanations of Vietnam. Indeed, it is the diversity of radical analyses of Vietnam that leads one radical critic, Staughton Lynd, to doubt whether "the Resistance should commit itself to a detailed explanation of the Vietnam war, which may not be possible for some time. . . ." Even so, Lynd entertains no doubt that "the Resistance should explicitly condemn capitalism as the ultimate source of America's aggressive foreign policy" or that "to oppose Vietnam without opposing capitalism is to acquiesce in future Vietnams."[5] It is the insistence upon finding the ultimate source of Vietnam in forces generated by American capitalism that gives radical critics their cohesiveness.

*   *   *

The focus of this essay is restricted to the central themes of the radical critique. In consequence, there are some aspects of this critique that are only touched upon and other aspects that are omitted entirely. The radical indictment of American diplomacy, past and present, is a very detailed one. To deal with it in anything resembling a thorough manner would require a very large volume. Even to examine the many issues radical historiography raises with respect to the origins of the cold war would prove a formidable and certainly a lengthy task. Within the compass of an essay, selectivity is unavoidable.

At the same time, it is not necessary to examine the entire range of the radical critique in order to lay bare its essential features. Not only is radical criticism repetitive, there are elements of this criticism that may be presumed to follow from its essential features and that, for this reason, do not require separate attention. Thus if American foreign policy is rooted in the structural needs of American capitalism (or in what America's corporate leaders believe those needs to be), it scarcely seems necessary to in-

[5] Staughton Lynd, "The Movement: A New Beginning," *Liberation* (May, 1969), pp. 18–19.

quire into the identity of the group that ultimately determines whether the nation's foreign policy satisfies those needs. A ruling class may elicit or, when necessary, enforce a broader consensus and its goals may be shared by the bureaucracy charged with the administration of foreign policy, but the nature of the goals which fundamentally define policy is still determined by the ruling class. In the radical view, the substantial identification of this class with America's corporate leaders renders unnecessary and even misleading the attention paid by nonradical analysts of foreign policy to the structure of bureaucratic decision making. The radical critic rejects, as indeed he must, the emphasis others place on bureaucracy as an independent force in the determination of policy. Moreover, this rejection of the military that the liberal critic finds in the growing threat of the "military industrial" establishment, has no parallel in the radical critique. To the contrary, no one believes more than the radical in the reality of the supremacy of civil over military authority.

This essay is restricted in yet another sense. It makes no attempt to examine the variety of expressions by which radical opposition to American foreign policy has been manifested in recent years. It is not an analysis of a political movement but of the thought that has partially informed a movement. Accordingly, it concentrates on the few who write books rather than on the many who seek to influence society through example and speech. In any age, the written word seems to be the least effective means of influence. In the present age, this relative impotence of the written word is more apparent than ever. In and of itself, the literature of radical left criticism did not evoke, and could not have evoked, a skeptical outlook toward American foreign policy. It is evidently the case that this skepticism was evoked primarily by events. Still, once events created the occasion for skepticism, the radical critique provided a response that seemed to many at least as persuasive as alternative responses. Not only did it appear to explain an otherwise inexplicable war, it related that war to a grand strategy that has presumably dominated American diplomacy throughout the century. In this manner, radical criticism came to exert in recent years an unexpected influence, particularly among the younger generation. How considerable that influence has been, and whether it may be expected to decline in the aftermath of Vietnam, are questions to which we shall return by way of conclusion. That it has already influenced the thought of a generation of students cannot be doubted. For this reason alone, radical criticism deserves attention.

Radical criticism also deserves attention by virtue of the light it throws on a more conventional criticism of American diplomacy. Indeed, the emergent influence of a radical critique must be regarded, in some measure at least, as a function of the adequacy—or inadequacy—of a conventional critique. The evident strength of radical criticism is to be found in its insistence upon the self-interested character of American foreign policy. By contrast, the dominant historiography since World War II has found in American foreign policy a rather consistent disregard of self-interest. For a conventional criticism, this inability to act consistently in terms of self-interest is at once the principal defect and the saving virtue of American diplomacy. In opposition to this theme, the radical critic may and does exaggerate the consistency of American efforts in this century to construct and

19

maintain a world order conducive to the power and prosperity of the United States. But even in exaggerating these efforts he has shown that the emphasis of a conventional historiography is scarcely credible.

The question remains whether a radical critique in properly calling our attention to the self-interested character of American foreign policy has done so for the right reasons. Even if it has not, as is argued in these pages, its influence on a conventional historiography may still prove considerable. Even if radical criticism betrays old illusions about the nature and sources of interest, it may still effect a substantial revision of conventional views. This revision is already apparent in the changes that have been made in what was once the accepted view of how the cold war arose. At any rate, a brief comparison of conventional and radical historiography is useful in pointing up the contrast between the two and thereby in illuminating the distinctive features of the radical position.

II. CONVENTIONAL AND RADICAL CRITIQUES OF AMERICAN FOREIGN POLICY

The dominant post-war interpretation of American diplomacy is not lacking in criticism. On the contrary, what may be termed the liberal-realist view of twentieth-century American foreign policy is, in its distinctive manner, quite pervasively critical. In this historiography, the American diplomatic record is marked by confusion and uncertainty over the ends and means of foreign policy, indeed, over the very nature and meaning of foreign policy. Whether it is the period of the Spanish-American War, the early vagaries of our Far Eastern policy, the debates preceding and following World War I, the struggle over American intervention in World War II, or the evolution of cold war policy, this essential theme persists. Our oscillation between isolationism and globalism, between indiscriminate withdrawal and indiscriminate involvement, our insistence upon defining foreign policy in sweeping ideological terms and viewing it as a contest between good and evil, our refusal to accept that rivalry and strife are the normal conditions of nations and of relations among nations, and above all, perhaps, our conviction that American wants and values are universal—these characteristic features of American diplomacy testify to our failure to understand the nature of statecraft. They underline what has been a profoundly unpolitical approach to foreign policy, incapable of making the kind of discriminating judgments that is the essence of a suc-

21

cessful statecraft. They explain why we have lacked, for the most part, a clear, consistent, and viable view of America's role and interests in the world. To be sure, there are by common agreement exceptions to this otherwise uninspiring record. But these exceptions—for example, the early years of containment—only serve to place in sharper relief the larger record of American diplomatic ineptitude.

Given this general assessment, the question must arise: How did we nevertheless manage to do so well? For if the by now conventionally critical interpretation is correct, the fact remains that seldom, if ever, in history has ineptitude and misunderstanding paid off with such handsome results. America's rise to world preponderance has not only been swift, it has been—at least, until recently—relatively painless. If this striking disparity between quality of effort and result must be explained, there is no apparent reason why it should not be put down simply to good fortune—above all, to the unique natural advantages America has enjoyed. That, at any rate, is the explanation a conventional critique is forced to take. The success we have enjoyed has come almost despite our conscious efforts, confused, inconsistent, and divorced from reality as presumably they have been.

It is this general theme that dominates the liberal-realist interpretation of American expansion in the twentieth century. The prevailing historiography dismisses, perhaps too self-consciously, a naive nationalism that would find in this expansion the reward of virtue or the design of Providence or the fulfillment of duty. Nor is America's expansion seen as a kind of "natural" process whereby power has created its own interests, the latter expanding in rough proportion to the former.[1] On the contrary, what impresses most observers about America's expansion in this century is precisely the opposite—that is, the disparity between power and interests. Thus it is argued that for most of the period in question our power has been disproportionate to our interests. When this has not been the case, as in the very recent period, our interests have been disproportionate to our power. This is but another way of saying that we have oscillated between isolationism and globalism, between indiscriminate withdrawal and indiscriminate involvement. Whatever the merit of the argument, it clearly rejects the view that the fact of American expansion in itself needs no special explanation.

Yet it is not easy to provide a plausible interpretation of our expansion once the view is rejected that the American experience does not differ essentially from the experience of all great powers. For the alternative explanation is to account for America's expansion in terms of a reasonably coherent and consistent strategy of expansion, and this would evidently cut across the central theme that American policy in this century has been, for the most part, marked by confusion and uncertainty. What has been interpreted as a deep rooted desire to escape the world, whether this escapism takes the form of isolationism or globalism, would instead have to be seen largely as a

---

[1] An apparent exception is R. W. Van Alstyne's *The Rising American Empire* (1960). But Van Alstyne's work deals almost entirely with the period prior to this century. In his brief treatment of twentieth-century expansion, Van Alstyne breaks with his previous analysis. What appears prior to this century as a "behavior pattern characteristic of an ambitious and dynamic national state" (p. 9) becomes in the twentieth century a crusading national mission divorced from all rational considerations of interest.

matter of employing varying means in the pursuit of coherent and relatively unvarying ends. So, too, the great debates of this century over American foreign policy would have to be seen as debates which concerned tactical and not strategic issues. A conventional historiography will no more accept these conclusions than it will accept the premise on which they must be based.

Given this outlook, it is not surprising that the explanation of America's expansion appears as a variation of the well known explanation once offered for the acquisition of empire by Great Britain. If America's expansion did not occur in a fit of absent mindedness, it still occurred without forethought and design. "The American empire," one contemporary observer declares, "came into being by accident and has been maintained from a sense of benevolence. Nobody planned our empire. In fact nobody wanted it."[2] This judgment is made with respect to America's post World War II expansion. It may be found all the more applicable, however, with respect to American expansion in the period from the turn of the century to World War II. It is of course scarcely possible to apply such an explanation to America's expansion in the Western Hemisphere, for our hemispheric expansion is too evidently rooted in historic pronouncement and avowed interest. But this exception apart, the view of America's accidental world expansion has been generally accepted. It is accepted, whether explicitly or implicitly, in interpretations of America's end of the century expansion beyond this hemisphere. The very diversity of attempts to account for this expansion, when coupled with the ap-

---

[2] Ronald Steel, *Pax Americana* (1967), p. 15.

parent inconclusiveness of each particular interpretation, suggests that the sudden and short-lived turn to colonial expansion was, after all, something in the nature of an accident—a "great aberration" as a still more conventional historiography has termed it. In suddenly turning to colonial expansion—to formal empire—the nation broke with its past but did not betake its future. What may be said of our acquisition of the Philippines may also be said of the policy of the Open Door. If the possession of the Philippines violated an anti-imperial tradition, certainly an anti-imperial tradition outside this hemisphere, the policy of the Open Door violated the norm of abstention from political involvement in the rivalries of European Powers, or, for that matter, of Asian Powers, save in circumstances where American security compelled a contrary course. In the absence of a threat to security emanating from East Asia, no serious political involvement could be consistently pursued. Thus the events of the turn of the century and beyond appear at once accidental, in that they are not seen to reflect the nation's historical traditions or its enduring interests, yet meaningful because they are found indicative of a tendency toward obscurantism in policy.

What the events of the turn of the century appear to indicate, the experience of World War I and its aftermath is found to confirm. The confusion and uncertainty over America's interest in the war and its outcome testify to an obscurantism in policy that even a threat to America's security interests could not overcome. This obscurantism must account, in the liberal-realist view, not only for the public's failure to understand the true meaning of America's intervention in the war, it must also account for the withdrawal of America from active involvement in world politics once the war was over. In the absence of an appreciation of the interests requiring American intervention, post-war involvement could be expected only if the world conformed to the American vision of it. Woodrow Wilson is the authentic spokesman for this vision. By defining the world in terms that bore no more than a tangential relation to political reality, if indeed that, Wilson symbolized the nation's continued remoteness from the world. By demanding the transformation of the traditional system of state relations, Wilson also symbolized the nation's continued inability to relate itself effectively to the world. While the very force of self-interest ultimately impelled intervention, a resistent and alien world could only lead to withdrawal once victory in war had been achieved.

It is only in the circumstances attending the outbreak of World War II that the threat to America's security held out by a hostile power, or combination of powers, in control of Eurasia becomes apparent. Despite extended debate, these circumstances precluded a repetition of the confusion and uncertainty over America's interest in the war and its outcome that marked the preceding conflict. But if it is true that in the years following 1939 the historic bases of isolationism were finally overturned, it is not true that the necessary consequences following from objective developments were clearly drawn and effectively acted upon. If isolationism—or its interwar variant—was abandoned, the inescapability of coming to terms with the perennial problems of statecraft was not yet accepted. Although America had decided that it could no longer avoid the world, it still did not accept the world but hoped instead to transform it into its own image.

Thus in the liberal-realist critique, America entered the post World War II period without a clear and consistent view of the world or of America's role and interests in it. Aware that a policy of isolation was no longer desirable or possible, yet unable to break clearly from the outlook and style formed through the historic experience of isolation, America hesitated for a brief, though critically important, moment between its past and its future. That moment of indecision was successfully overcome only by virtue of the clarity of the Soviet-American confrontation in Europe and the importance of the interests at stake in that confrontation. But the hope that America might transform the world persisted despite the realism and success of the early policy of containment. Indeed, it was the very success of containment that helped reinvigorate an outlook that had never been abandoned and had been given quintessential expression in the Truman Doctrine. The triumph of the Truman Doctrine in policy describes the essential course of American diplomacy over the following two decades. What began as a policy largely limited to Europe, directed primarily against the expansion of Soviet power, and designed to restore a balance of power, ended as a policy unlimited in geographic scope, directed against communism itself, and designed to preserve a global status quo bearing little, if any, relation to the balance of power.

The history of American diplomacy since the early post-war period is accordingly seen in the liberal-realist critique not only as a history of decline from an initial clarity of concept to obscurantism, and from an initial modesty of action to a virtual compulsion for the disproportionate act, but also as a reminder of the extent to which the past continues to rule the present. Despite the global expansion of American power we have still to form a satisfactory and viable relation between that power and the nation's vital interests. But if American policy has been misguided, this is not to say that it has been malevolent. A conventional historiography may find our perceptions faulty, but it does not identify our perceptions with our intentions. It may find our judgment wanting, but our motives cannot be gainsaid; if we have misused our power, it is not through the desire to exploit others. The failure of American foreign policy is a failure compounded of sentimentality and intellectual error. The consequences may prove disastrous, as they have in Vietnam. Still, there is something akin to a saving grace that emerges from this analysis. Although a policy of misplaced altruism may lead to disaster, particularly when recipients are determined to resist American benevolence, it is still somehow redeemable precisely because of its essentially disinterested character.

* * *

It is only a slight exaggeration to say that the radical interpretation of American diplomacy appears as an inverted mirror image of liberal-realist historiography. Where the latter finds confusion and uncertainty, the former finds clarity and consistency. What is to the latter evidence of obscurantism in policy, is to the former confirmation of the highly rational character of policy. Whereas a conventional historiography emphasizes the role of the unforeseen, the contingent, and the inadvertent, a radical historiography leaves very little scope to these factors. The liberal-realist critic may give low grades to most American statesmen, but the radical critic takes a quite different view of their competence. If the men who guided the nation's diplomacy faithfully served the interests of American capitalism, this is not to say they were fools. To the contrary, they are considered, for the most part, as having been highly competent. (How else to explain the remarkable success of American diplomacy?) Certainly they were not bemused by an abstract moralism regularly attributed to them by liberal-realist critics.

In radical interpretations, then, there is no need to account for what appears in the dominant postwar interpretation as a striking disparity between quality of effort and result. Until very recently the American diplomatic record is judged a success by most radical historians. That this success carried within it from the start the seeds of failure and that this failure is now well upon us cannot detract from earlier triumphs. For a period of well over half a century American statesmen effectively pursued an expansionist strategy aimed at "stabilizing the world in a pro-American equilibrium"[3] and did so on the whole through methods congenial to American power and interests.

These traits of radical historiography are often held up by critics to imply a conspiratorial version of American foreign policy. The charge would appear to have little merit. It is true that radical historians find American statesmen pursuing a remarkably coherent and consistent strategy. But this view does not presuppose a conspiracy, unless we define as conspira-

[3] William A. Williams, *The Tragedy of American Diplomacy* (rev. ed., 1962), p. 299.

torial any sustained action that is coherent and consistent. That American statesmen are found to act in accord with the needs, whether real or assumed, of the American economy does not mark them as conspiratorial any more than does a description of American statesmen as acting in accord with the needs, whether real or assumed, of American security. Indeed, to the extent that radical historians find the actions of American statesmen determined by the inherent needs of America's socio-economic structure, the result would appear to be the very opposite of a conspiratorial interpretation, which is, par excellence, voluntaristic in character.

The distinctiveness of radical historiography must instead be found in the assumption that American diplomacy is essentially a response to forces generated by America's economic and social structure. This assumption accounts for the more familiar traits of radical historiography. Once it is granted, the striking continuity radical historians see in American diplomacy follows almost as a matter of course. The study of American diplomacy reveals debates over tactical issues; it does not reveal meaningful debates over issues of strategy. What a conventional historiography considers as great debates in this century, the outcome of which has determined the general direction of American policy, a radical historiography considers as little more than differences over the proper means for implementing unchanging ends. Thus the debates at the turn of the century on the annexation of Hawaii and the Philippines are found to reveal differences over how best to achieve America's expansion; they are not found to reveal differences over the need for such expansion. The belief that constantly expanding markets were indispensable to the economic and political well-being of the nation provided the starting point for both annexationists and anti-annexationists. And though the victory of the former was to prove something of an aberration, it was so not only, and perhaps not even primarily, because the assertion of direct control over noncontiguous territory and people violated American traditions, but because the circumstances in which America's world expansion occurred rendered the method of traditional colonialism increasingly unnecessary and inefficient. In an age witnessing the decline of the older imperialism, the policy formally enunciated with respect to China in the Open Door Notes at once avoided the burden and embarrassment, and inefficiency, of formal empire while establishing the conditions under which America's preponderant economic power could be effectively brought to bear on behalf of America's expansion.[4]

In radical historiography, the strategy of American expansion is given its classic formulation during the period of World War I. For both conventional and radical critics, Woodrow Wilson occupies a unique position since for both he is the authentic spokesman in this century of the nation's vision of itself in relation to the world. But whereas the liberal-realist critic finds that vision utopian in aspiration and lacking in appreciation of America's interests, the radical critic sees in the Wilsonian vision the

[4] Cf. William A. Williams, *The Tragedy of American Diplomacy*, pp. 16–84; Walter LaFeber, *The New Empire: An Interpretation of American Expansion, 1860–1898* (1963); and Lloyd C. Gardner, "American Foreign Policy 1900–1921: A Second Look at the Realist Critique of American Diplomacy," in *Towards a New Past: Dissenting Essays in American History* (1968), ed. by Barton J. Bernstein, pp. 202–31.

faithful and consistent expression of liberal-capitalist internationalism. As such, it was neither utopian in vision nor lacking in appreciation of America's interests. Its universalism might testify to its potentially unlimited aspirations; it does not testify to a lack of realism about the nature of interest itself. For Wilsonian universalism never failed to equate the triumph of liberal-capitalist internationalism with the economic and political interests of the principal guarantor of this order. And if the ultimate failures of the Wilsonian vision are apparent, the radical judgment remains that the strategy it marked out led to the extension of American economic and political power throughout the world.

The significance of Wilsonianism, then, is that it "defined the American national interest in liberal-internationalist terms in response to war and revolution, the two dominant political factors of our time."[5] The policy of the Open Door presupposed from the start a stable world order of liberal-capitalist internationalism, the leadership of which would eventually gravitate to the United States. As the events of 1914–18 made clear, however, this order was threatened both by traditional imperialism, with its attendant evils of militarism and war, and by revolutionary socialism. A world made safe from both threats was accordingly Wilson's ultimate aim, as it was to be the ultimate aim of his successors. But if Wilson

---

[5] N. Gordon Levin, Jr., *Woodrow Wilson and World Politics: America's Response to War and Revolution* (1968), p. 2. Levin's detailed and subtle interpretation of Wilson's thought and strategy is, on essential points, similar to the interpretation of Wilson given by Williams in *The Tragedy of American Diplomacy*. For a more general view, see Arno J. Mayer, *Politics and Diplomacy of Peacemaking: Containment and Counterrevolution at Versailles, 1918–1919* (1968).

sought to change the international system, in the radical view the nature and scope of that change remained limited. The new diplomacy Wilson called for did not question the continued predominance of the West. What it did insist on was a change in the forms by which this predominance would henceforth be expressed and preserved. That the new forms were particularly congenial to America's economic and political expansion, Wilson saw as a felicitous, though of course not unmerited, coincidence. Even so, the bias in Wilson's new diplomacy hardly reveals him as a statesman who sought to substitute abstract moral principle for America's expansionist goals. He simply expressed these goals in a form congenial to himself and to the nation.

For the radicals, the debate over the League of Nations must be understood as a disagreement over the proper tactics for implementing the strategic goals of American policy. A small minority apart, these goals were not seriously questioned. What was questioned was the wisdom and desirability of attempting to realize them through the League of Nations. For Wilson, the triumph of a liberal-capitalist world order under America's leadership required that the international system be reformed from within. But Wilson's league was no utopian order divorced from interest. If it disavowed the traditional system of diplomacy and called for a new system of state relations in which a balance of power and its inevitable concomitant, alliances, would be replaced by a community of power, it did so out of the conviction that such reformation was in the interests not only of America but of the other Capitalist powers, victorious and defeated alike.

The eventual defeat of the league was therefore a partial rejection of the Wilsonian plan for implementing the policy of American expansion, not a rejection of the policy itself. It is not the triumph of isolationism that emerges from the debate over the league but the triumph of unilateralism. For both the left and the right, the league threatened to involve America in the wars of Europe and, by tying us to the peace settlement, to make the United States an instrument of the Allied powers. In rejecting that prospect the nation did not opt for isolationism but for retaining inviolate America's freedom of action. Yet the ends for which America's economic and political power would be employed remained unchanged. The Wilsonian ends—America's economic and political expansion within a liberal-internationalist order which would be both cause and consequence of this expansion—continued to express the essence of American foreign policy.

Given these ends, America's isolationism in the interwar period is in radical historiography a myth. A conventional historiography perpetuates this myth because it identifies isolationism with an unwillingness to form alliances and to rely upon military power as the principal means of policy. If this identification is resisted, American policy appears as anything but isolationist. The refusal to form alliances did not signify a refusal to enter into a concert of policy with the major industrial powers having as its objectives the containment of the Soviet Union (and revolutionary movements generally) and the orderly development of the nonindustrialized regions according to the principles of the Open Door. Nor did the refusal to rely upon military power signify an inability to relate interest and power. What it did presumably signify was a profound fear of war as the harbinger of revolution abroad and repression at home and, of course, the conviction that America's economic preponderance made the reliance on military power unnecessary in the pursuit of the nation's interests.

The events of the 1930s eventually undermined that conviction, though they did not alter the interests conviction expressed. If anything, a persisting economic stagnation at home only made those interests appear more vital than ever. Prosperity and democracy required more than ever the assurance of a world made safe for America's economic and political expansion. Could such a world be assured by the preferred methods of the Open Door? The question, in the radical view, goes to the heart of the debate of the late thirties—a debate which, once again, concerned the means not the ends of policy. America's leaders were, on the whole, profoundly opposed to war. Yet they were even more profoundly committed to goals which, it became increasingly apparent, could no longer be secured except by war. In the end, the substantial decision for war—though not the immediate precipitant of war—was the inevitable consequence, after a series of abortive attempts at compromise with the Axis Powers, of the long standing commitment to the goals of the Open Door.[6]

The same goals are found to determine the course of American diplomacy during and following World

---

[6] Cf. Lloyd C. Gardner, *Economic Aspects of New Deal Diplomacy* (1964), who is in essential agreement with the thesis elaborated by Williams in *The Tragedy of American Diplomacy*. For the application of a similar view to the conflict between America and Japan, see Noam Chomsky, *American Power and the New Mandarins* (1969), pp. 159–220.

War II. The circumstances attending the war and immediate post-war period did not alter the expansionist policy America had pursued for decades. On the contrary, the traumatic experience of the thirties and the persistent fear of its recurrence in the post-war period only intensified the determination to ensure that the post-war world would be so constituted as to serve the functional needs of American capitalism. To an even greater degree than before, these needs were seen in terms of America's foreign economic expansion and, in consequence, of an international environment receptive to such expansion. Moreover, the determination to reconstruct the world economy according to American needs and desires, a task that would evidently require an appropriate political structure, was now matched by a power preponderance almost without parallel in modern history—a preponderance of which the atomic bomb seemed to be the ultimate symbol. In contrast to World War I, this time America would reshape the international system from within and would do so from a position of preponderant power. It is in essence a re-enforced and more aggressive Wilsonian version of a stable world order of liberal-capitalist internationalism under American leadership and control that emerges in radical historiography as America's dominant war aim.[7]

To the radical historian, then, the origins of the cold war are clear. Given the essential thrust of American policy, conflict with the Soviet Union was unavoidable. For that policy not only led to implaca-

[7] The radical interpretation of America's wartime diplomacy is most fully—and, one must add, implacably—developed in Gabriel Kolko's *The Politics of War: The World and United States Foreign Policy, 1943–1945* (1968).

ble opposition to the left everywhere, and particularly in Europe, and to an insistence upon linking all revolutionary forces to Soviet inspiration and control, it also led to the determined effort to restore everywhere the old order—or, at best, a modestly reformed version of the old order. In Western Europe this effort incurred no opposition from the Soviet Union until the cold war was fully joined. Instead, the Soviets, intent upon avoiding an open break with its Western Allies, while realizing their limited security aims in Eastern Europe, initially cooperated with the United States and Great Britain by restraining the large western Communist parties and, indeed, by bidding them to join in the endeavor to restore the old order. Even in Eastern Europe, it is argued, the Soviet Union gave every sign of willingness to distinguish between a sphere of influence and a sphere of domination and, provided only that they were not anti-Soviet, to content themselves with the establishment of neutralist regimes of varying complexion. If the Soviets came in time to make Eastern Europe into a sphere of domination, the radical argument is that American policy brought about this result by its reluctance to concede what were initially quite modest and conservative Soviet claims in Eastern Europe, by its refusal to afford the Soviets any reliable assurance against a renascent Germany, and, finally, by its active challenge to the entire Soviet post-war position in Europe.

That American leaders so acted because they believed Soviet action in Eastern Europe was a serious threat to Western Europe's security, hence to America's security, is variously treated by radical critics. It is of course the common currency among them to dismiss the possibility, let alone the plausibility, that the belief could have had any objective basis. Quite apart from the presumably limited aims of Soviet policy in Europe, the vast superiority of power America is held to have enjoyed during these years must rule out any serious security problem.[8] Even so, some do not deny, if only by implication, that America's anticommunism was something more than an ideological mask for American imperialism. If we found dangers to our security where none existed, this is occasionally explained in terms of a paranoia that was matched, on the other extreme, only by our hubris. Thus an exaggerated fear of leftist revolutions, invariably directed by and subservient to the Soviet Union, which would jeopardize capitalism as a world system, and American capitalism along with it, was combined with an equally exaggerated faith in our ability to control events everywhere and construct a stable world order cast in a pro-American equilibrium.

In the main, however, it is the consciously deliberate character of American policy in the years during and immediately following World War II that is emphasized in radical historiography. Hegemonial in aim, this policy can be attributed neither to chance (in the radical *weltanschauung* nothing of significance happens by chance) nor to the alleged compulsions of the international system (America's preponderant power freed it from any external compulsions).

[8] This point is central to radical historiography of the cold war. Williams makes it the starting point for an understanding of the cold war and draws from it the lesson of America's primary responsibility for the conflict. "For power and responsibility go together in a direct and intimate relationship." *The Tragedy of American Diplomacy*, p. 208. See also Walter La Feber, *America, Russia, and the Cold War, 1945–1966* (1968), for a more moderate statement of essentially the same point.

However inferior the power position of the Soviet Union at the end of the war, when compared with the position of the United States, it had no alternative to resisting a strategy which, if successful, would not only have deprived it of the fruits of victory but of a physical security for which it had paid an enormous price.

The resulting conflict with the Soviet Union is only one of the consequences found to have attended a strategy intent upon establishing an integrated world capitalism under American direction and control. In the long run, most radicals believe, it is of greater significance that American policy committed the nation to attempt to preserve, with minimally necessary reforms, the old order everywhere. Only in the industrialized states of Western Europe and Japan did the attempt succeed. Elsewhere, the circumstances marking the early years of the cold war only succeeded in momentarily arresting a broad movement toward revolutionary change that must ultimately have a far greater impact on the international system, and on the American position in this system, than did the Bolshevik Revolution and the subsequent growth of Soviet power. Even in this earlier period, however, and in uniquely favorable circumstances, the nature of American goals threatened to exceed our capacities. For those goals could only be implemented, in the words of one radical historian, by setting the United States "against the Soviet Union, against the tide of the left, and against Britain as a coequal guardian of world capitalism—in fact, against history as it had been and had yet to become."[9]

* * *

[9] Kolko, *The Politics of War*, pp. 624–25.

In their interpretations of American diplomacy since the early post-war years, there are apparent points of convergence between radical and liberal-realist critics. Both see the later history of American diplomacy as one of growing frustration with and apprehension over a world that is increasingly resistant to American interests and power. Both insist that American policy has become increasingly repressive in method and obsessively counterrevolutionary in aim. For both, a policy of global intervention must fail since it must result in the over-extension of American power.

But these apparent points of convergence only cover deeper disagreement. A conventional critique finds in the decline of post-war American diplomacy the steady erosion and, indeed, the perversion of a policy which, in origin, was not only modest in aim but progressive and liberating in character. To the liberal-realist critic, contemporary globalism, the gradual universalization of the Truman Doctrine in the realm of policy, is the very antithesis of the early policy of containment, with its focus on Europe and its principal objective of restoring a balance of power. With its indiscriminate commitment to intervene anywhere and everywhere against revolutionary change, globalism substitutes sentiment and ideology for interest, imaginary fears for what were in an earlier period well-grounded fears. It reflects a view of the world that is profoundly at odds with the reality of a pluralistic world, that has resulted in the overcommitment of the nation's resources, and that if not abandoned must betray the American purpose both abroad and at home.

What the liberal-realist critics see as the perversion of earlier policy, the radicals find as the consistent and inevitable outcome of earlier policy. To the latter, globalism, itself a euphemism for America's hegemony in the world, has been throughout the overriding aim of American policy. And if America's globalism has led today to Vietnam and threatens to lead tomorrow to still graver crises, there is little reason for believing that this overriding aim will be abandoned. Now more than ever globalism is not a matter of choice but a necessity. For the dangers a liberal-realist critique labels as imaginary are indeed real. The world is increasingly resistant to America's hegemonial position. Yet America, more dependent than ever on this position, has little choice but to defend it, however great the risks that defense may entail.

In the radical view, then, a conventional critique obscures the essential consistency of America's postwar policy by obscuring the interests on behalf of which this policy has been pursued. Insistent upon the initially limited character of American interests in the post-war period, a conventional historiography defines those interests primarily in terms of the presumed threat to American security resulting from the post-war weakness and instability of Europe.

Given this interpretation of the early period of containment, and thereby of the origins of the cold war as well, the liberal-realist judgment of the subsequent "decline" of American policy becomes readily understandable. What is found initially to have been a political struggle fought for real stakes, for vital national interests, is found subsequently to have been transformed into an ideological contest, involving illusory—or, at best, only marginal—stakes. Precipitated in large measure by Korea, the spread of the cold war beyond Europe thus marks for conventional historiography the great watershed in post-war American diplomacy. In the place of a policy initially designed to restore and maintain a balance of power, there emerged a policy that bore little, if any, relation to the balance of power. Universalist in aspiration and committed to the maintenance of the status quo there is no real continuity between this policy and its predecessor. A conventional critique not only concludes that America's post-war diplomacy has been marked by discontinuity but that the discontinuity cannot be explained in terms of any rational calculation of interest. If American security and well-being cannot be seriously jeopardized by revolutionary change in the underdeveloped world (at least, if it cannot be seriously jeopardized by any change that it is plausible to expect), if the economic advantages drawn from policy are outweighed by the costs of policy, and if hegemony for the sake of hegemony is ruled out, there remains no apparently rational motivation for policy. At least, there remains no apparently self-interested motivation for policy. Instead, what remains are largely disinterested and, as it turns out, quite humane motives (attachment to self-determination, resistance to aggression, etc.). Even the desire to see the world emulate America becomes, on this view, a disinterested, if misguided, motive. Once again, then, we are back to the theme that the failure of American foreign policy is a failure compounded of sentimentality and intellectual error.

A radical critique can no more accept this judgment than it can accept the judgment of discontinuity in post-war policy. What conventional critics see as discontinuity, radical critics see as no more than successive phases of the same strategy of establishing an integrated Capitalist world order under American direction and control. In the pursuit of this strategy, Western Europe came first not because its physical security was threatened by the Soviet Union but because the restoration of stable Capitalist regimes was indispensable to the success of the strategy. Nor did the spectre of Communist accession to power in Western Europe threaten America's physical security. It did clearly threaten the American strategy for the post-war world, and by so doing, it threatened what American leaders considered to be essential to the nation's post-war prosperity and well-being. Western Europe came first in the priorities of America's post-war diplomacy because it was there that the first great threat to America's global strategy developed. The later spread of the cold war beyond Europe—itself a misleading way, in the radical view, of putting the matter—is therefore not a perversion of earlier policy but its logical progression. In the subsequent shift of focus from Europe to Asia, and to the world at large, American strategy found its fulfillment.

At issue here are not only widely different interpretations of the cold war but almost different meanings given to the term itself. In conventional historiography, American foreign policy until the 1960s is equated with the cold war. In turn, the essence of the cold war is defined as the conflict with the Soviet Union for the control of Western Europe. We may have endowed that conflict from the start with an excessively ideological character and confused Russian imperialism with international communism, but the interpretation remains substantially unimpaired. Even in the years following Korea, when the cold war had generated a momentum of its own, when its theatre had expanded far beyond Europe, and when, in consequence of this expansion, its stakes had evidently changed considerably, it is still a hegemonial Soviet-American rivalry that presumably continues to define the cold war and American policy generally. Only with the passing of the Cuban missile crisis, the last great crisis in Soviet-American relations, does the cold war abate, if it does not disappear, to be succeeded by a crisis which, despite its origins in the cold war, bears little objective relationship to this earlier conflict. It bears little objective relationship to this earlier conflict, in part, because the parties involved have changed and, in part, because the nature of the interests at stake are presumably of a different order.

In radical historiography, however, the cold war was always a part of a much larger conflict that followed from the nature of American aims. Those aims not only set America at odds with the Soviet Union but inevitably with most of the rest of the world as well, for they amounted to the claim of a right to determine the course of development of most of the world. The principal significance of the post-war conflict with the Soviet Union (and still later with China) is that it provided the opportunity to consolidate and to further America's expansion. What a conventional historiography defines as the essence of the cold war is instead essentially the institutionalization of American expansion—that is, the creation of the vast economic, political, and military "infrastructure" of America's global empire. This empire is no accident, no unintended by-product, of our conflict with the Soviet Union (and later with China). It comprised the principal occasion for, as well as the central goal of, that conflict. In the substitution of "world order" for "containment," and in the equation of world order with American security, the contemporary litany of American foreign policy is held to provide oblique acknowledgment of this interpretation.

The period of the cold war is therefore in the radical view the period of the final stage of development of the American empire. In sheer magnitude as well as in the development of institutional forms of control, it is the period of greatest growth. Yet it is also the period marked, on the one hand, by America's ever increasing dependence on the empire and, on the other hand, by an ever growing resistance to America by the empire. This apparent paradox of dependence in strength, together with a growing resistance to that strength, goes to the heart of the radical analysis of the contemporary crisis in American foreign policy. It also accounts for the insistence that the present crisis is, both in nature and scope, almost qualitatively different from earlier crises. Whereas even a generation ago the aim of an integrated world Capitalist order directed and controlled by America was still in large measure unfulfilled, today it is a reality. Yet this very success, together with all of the consequences success has wrought, defines for the radical the nature of the present crisis, while differentiating it from earlier crises in American diplomacy. It is no longer the fear, mistaken or otherwise, of what might happen to America's institutions if we are compelled to forego expansion but the well-grounded fear of what will happen if we are forced to relinquish what we presently hold. For the prosperity and cohesiveness of the American system as constituted today are dependent upon retaining control over an integrated world Capitalist order. Without this control America could no longer be assured of continued access on favorable terms to the raw materials necessary to sustain present levels of production and consumption, let alone still higher levels. Without this control, the present patterns of world market relationships would no longer be secure. Finally, without this control not only would existing foreign investment be jeopardized but the very option of foreign investment, so vital to a Capitalist economy, could no longer be assured. In sum, our security in the broader sense, the security of the American system as it is presently constituted, has become dependent upon meeting and defeating any challenges to our imperial position.

Given this dependence, our obsession with stability is understandable. For America's security in the greater than physical sense has become increasingly inseparable from a stability which is little more than a synonym for the status quo. If the status quo must generate resistance, America, as the principal beneficiary and guarantor of the status quo, has little option but to put down resistance. A policy of global intervention is not a matter of choice, then, but of necessity. It can be abandoned only at the risk—tantamount to a certainty—of abandoning the hegemonial position America has occupied since World War II.

*   *   *

Nowhere is the contrast between the conventional and radical criticisms more clearly illustrated than in the respective interpretations of Vietnam. To the liberal-realist critic, Vietnam stands out above all else as a failure of political intelligence. In part, it is true, the catastrophe of Vietnam is explained in terms of chance, bad luck, and the accident of personality, just as in part it is explained in terms of the inadequacies of the institutions by which the nation conducts its foreign policy. But these factors, it is generally conceded, although significant, do not go to the heart of the matter. Beyond inadvertance, bureaucratic inertia and vested interests, the idiosyncracies of presidents and their advisors, and simple bad luck, there is a larger policy—and, even more important, a persistent style or outlook—that made Vietnam an ever-present possibility. That policy, as we have already seen, grew out of the earlier conflict with the Soviet Union. Vietnam is therefore the legacy of the cold war (particularly the Asian legacy), of the momentum generated by the cold war, and of the habits of throught and action that the cold war encouraged.

But if the habits of thought and action which led to Vietnam were encouraged by the cold war, they did not stem simply from that conflict. At the heart of the liberal-realist explanation of Vietnam is a style of thought and of action that has its roots deep in the American past. What Vietnam reveals is what the modern American diplomatic record as a whole reveals. The distinctiveness and significance of Vietnam is that it reveals the salient and persistent characteristics of American diplomacy in intensely magnified form. In Vietnam, the consequences to which our ingrained misconceptions can lead, when unfavorable circumstances so combine to produce a kind of limiting case, appear as perhaps they have never appeared before.

At the same time, if Vietnam is seen as a limiting case it is also seen as a tragic one. What makes Vietnam tragic, above and beyond the consequences which always attend war, is the judgment that our motives and intentions were good and our objectives worthy. That these intentions and objectives were flawed by a host of misconceptions—about the nature and requirements of American security, about the nature of large-scale insurrections and the difficulty of putting them down at acceptable cost by outside intervention, about the specific political realities in Vietnam—is perfectly true, but that does not alter the judgment on the objectives we sought and our intent in seeking them.

The tragedy of Vietnam, then, consists in the disparity between intentions and objectives, on the one side, and our behavior as well as the results of our behavior, on the other side. However good our intentions and however worthy our objectives, given the political realities in Vietnam we have fought a war in which success was all but precluded from the start. To the extent that success was ever a meaningful prospect it was so only by using means which, if they did not jeopardize the ends we sought, were disproportionately costly. Thus in the liberal-realist critique the disparity which defines the tragedy of Vietnam also defines the immorality of the war. Even so, there is something akin to a saving grace that emerges from this critique, just as there is something akin to a saving grace that emerges from the general liberal-realist critique of American diplomacy. If Vietnam has led to disaster and tragedy, and ultimately even to immorality, we may still in a way redeem Vietnam, and ourselves, if only we are able to appreciate and to correct the misconceptions the war so clearly revealed.[10]

[10] No brief summary can pretend to encompass the varied criticisms non-radical critics have made of Vietnam. At best, it can do no more than indicate the central thrust of this criticism, and particularly the criticism here termed liberal-realist. Perhaps the most cogent expression of the latter is to be found among the majority of the contributors to *No More Vietnams? The War and the Future of American Foreign Policy* (1968), edited by Richard M. Pfeffer.

Whereas the liberal-realist critique finds in Vietnam the consequences to which a defective political intelligence may lead, the radical critique finds in Vietnam a preview of the consequences to which American imperialism must lead. America's Vietnam policy, a popular radical tract reads, "does not merely illustrate American imperialism, it is a paradigm instance of it . . . . [In] its fusion of imperialist motive and anticommunist ideology, the war is not only exemplary, it is also climactic."[11] In Vietnam the mask that has so long concealed the true character of American policy has been torn away and the lengths to which American power will be employed to defeat a social revolution found to threaten America's hegemonial position have been fully revealed. These circumstances alone would make the crisis resulting from Vietnam unparalleled, for they have made transparently clear the hypocrisy of America's professed ideals. The crisis is immeasurably intensified, however, by the prospect of a *dénouement* in which either Vietnam must be destroyed or America must accept a barely disguised defeat. Even a cautious projection of the international and domestic effects of either outcome indicates the unprecedented nature of the crisis.

The problem of Vietnam can no more be understood in terms of chance, inadvertance, or the accident of personality, than it can be understood in terms of the misconceptions—the intellectual errors —of policy makers. To see Vietnam in terms of contingent factors is to deprive a momentous event in world history of rational meaning and significance. To see Vietnam as the result of misconceptions is to

---

[11] Carl Oglesby, "Vietnamese Crucible," in *Containment and Change*, by Oglesby and Schaull (1967), pp. 112–13.

deny, if only by implication, that the motive force of American policy is to be found in the institutional structure of American society and the interests this structure must generate. Moreover, once this view is accepted the way is opened to concluding that whatever the "mistakes" of policy and however unfortunate, even disastrous, the consequences of these mistakes, a distinction may, and in the American case should, still be drawn between intentions and behavior, between objectives and results. Other states may be driven by interests but we are driven by good intentions, however deeply rooted these intentions may be in misconceptions about the world and America's relationship to the world. The result is invariably a partial justification of American policy and a partial exoneration of our sins.[12]

To the radical critic, this same tendency to obscure the real roots of the war, while serving as a subtle kind of justification for what we have done, is apparent in the view that Vietnam is a legacy of the cold war. For the view that Vietnam is a legacy of the cold war evidently implies that Vietnam must be considered as an unfortunate hangover of the excesses and rigidities to which this earlier conflict finally gave rise. Once again we are back to the conventional critique of the cold war, discussed in preceding pages, though now applied to Vietnam. Once again the radical response is to insist that Vietnam is

[12] Among radical critics, perhaps none has been more insistent on this point than Noam Chomsky. Chomsky's *American Power and the New Mandarins* is a detailed criticism of "the kind of sentimentality that sees the United States, alone among nations, as a selfless (if rather oafish) public benefactor, devoted only to projects of 'international good will,' though frequently blundering in an excess of warmhearted generosity" (p. 312).

50

the result of a policy we have consistently pursued throughout the post World War II period. Given this policy and its overriding aim, a Vietnam was sooner or later inevitable, since ultimately there is no way to ensure control over the course of development of the Third World other than by military intervention. This is not to deny Vietnam has been a gigantic piece of bad luck and that had America's leaders known of the difficulties they would face in Vietnam they would have refrained from intervening (at any rate, on such a massive scale) and sought instead more appropriate terrain in which to establish a precedent-setting victory over radical revolution. It is to deny that Vietnam is an aberration or accident in the sense that America's imperial interests permit us to avoid incurring the constant risk, and eventually the certainty, of Vietnams. If American policy is interventionist, and if this interventionism was destined eventually to encounter a Vietnam, it is because of the nature of American interests and, of course, the nature of the world in which those interests must be realized.

In the broader sense, then, Vietnam is no failure of political intelligence, as a liberal-realist critique would have it. Vietnam was perceived, and rightly so, as a threat to America's imperial structure, whether directly in Southeast Asia or indirectly in the world at large. Given the nature of American interests, the decision to respond by armed intervention was not unreasonable. It was not unreasonable to assume that a failure to respond to the challenge in Vietnam would encourage others to challenge the order over which America presides. Moreover, it was not unreasonable to assume that a failure to respond to the challenge in Vietnam would call into question

the justification of large military expenditures. The
critical military sector of the economy, dependent as
always upon its anti-Communist rationale, had to be
vindicated. For once, the justification was not a hoax.
The threat held out by Vietnam was real. It was not
America's physical security that was threatened,
but the security of an economic and social system dependent upon the fruits conferred by America's hegemonial position. A world in which others controlled
the course of their own development, and America's
hegemonial position was broken, would be a world in
which the American system itself would be seriously
endangered. To prevent this prospect from materializing, to reveal to others what they can expect if they
seek to control the course of their own development,
the United States intervened in Vietnam.

Can we afford to get out of Vietnam if getting out
must mean the acceptance of a barely disguised defeat? If the interests in defense of which we presumably intervened were indeed vital, is it possible
to abandon the field now without incurring inordinate risks? Must not these risks prove even greater
today than they were at the time of intervention
when American power and prestige were not yet so
massively committed? These questions do not elicit
a uniform response from radical critics. To some, defeat in Vietnam can have no other result than to reveal the limits of American power and to do so in
such a way as to jeopardize the entire structure of
our imperial order. For the United States to fail in
Vietnam, after so massive an intervention, cannot
but call into question the system we have both created and guaranteed. It is trivial, even if true, to
argue in retrospect that the intervention was a mistake, that Vietnam was not the place to respond to

52

the challenge of revolutionary change. What is important today is not what might have been done but what has been done and, of course, what may, or must, be expected to happen if the American intervention in Vietnam fails.[13] To others, unwilling to pursue this logic to its extreme, Vietnam can be abandoned and though it is agreed that the consequences of defeat will be serious it is nevertheless argued that the imperial system will survive.[14] For those who take the latter view, the liabilities, domestic and international, attending a continuation of the war have finally become so great that the enterprise will have to be liquidated.

This disagreement is significant in that it reflects varying judgments on the strength of the imperial system, the potentialities for revolutionary movements in the Third World, and even the degree of dependence on the advantages conferred by empire. It also reflects varying judgments on the determination of those who govern America to have their way,

[13] Thus Gabriel Kolko writes: "For the United States to fail in Vietnam would be to make the point that even the massive intervention of the most powerful nation in the history of the world was insufficient to stem profoundly popular social and national revolutions throughout the world. Such a revelation of American weaknesses would be tantamount to a demotion of the United States from its present role as the world's dominant superpower." *The Roots of American Foreign Policy* (1969), p. 90. Moreover, with that demotion, the United States would become increasingly isolated in a hostile world and "American prosperity within its present social framework would dry up" (pp. 85–86).—In its essential structure, there is an obvious parallel between this view and the view entertained by the fervent defenders of Vietnam.

[14] Noam Chomsky has written that "this particular venture [Vietnam] could no doubt be liquidated without too severe a blow to the system." *Liberation* (August-September 1969), p. 39.

53

whatever the domestic costs and effects, just as it reflects varying judgments on the potential of domestic forces of resistance. Even so, it does not affect the essential consensus among radicals on the basic causes of the war. Nor does it affect the view that Vietnam represents an unparalleled crisis for American imperialism. In revealing the true nature of American policy, Vietnam has also exposed the limits to America's ability to suppress national liberation movements. Eventually, the example set by Vietnam will be emulated by others and the difficulties attending Vietnam will again appear, though in a still more acute form. The alternatives before us, then, are clear. Either America must prepare for a never-ending conflict that it cannot reasonably expect to win despite its immense power, a conflict in the course of which it must give up even the pretense of democracy at home, or it must accept a fundamentally different relationship with the world. Given the transformation of American society the latter alternative would necessitate, in the radical view, the prospects for its occurrence must remain at best uncertain.

How are we to assess the radical left's critique of American foreign policy? The answer obviously depends upon how we understand the critique. If we see it as little more than an account of the expansion of American power and influence, then much of its distinctiveness is lost. (This is so even if such expansion is invariably equated, as it is in the radical critique, with imperialism.) To be sure, the insistence that expansion is the essence of the American tradition in foreign policy is far more pronounced in radical history than in more conventional critiques. Nevertheless, expansion is a theme that may accommodate and has accommodated otherwise diverse views of American diplomacy. If the radical view is distinctive, it is not primarily because of its emphasis upon expansion, or even because of its account of the manner in which expansion occurred, but because of its explanation of why we have been so persistently expansionist and, of course, of what we have sought to obtain through expansion.

Yet a closer examination of radical interpretations of American diplomacy does not reveal unanimity on these critical issues. The consensus among radical critics that expansion has been *the* principle of our institutions and the dominant characteristic of the American tradition in foreign policy has not precluded differences from arising over the sources of our inveterate habit of aggrandizement. Must this expansion be seen fundamentally as the result of institutional necessity? Or may it be seen largely as the result of what America's leaders—and, to a large extent, the public as well—have mistakenly believed to be the needs of our institutions?

These questions receive no uniform answers from radical historians. To some, they are turned aside as irrelevant. To others, however, they are dealt with in an ambiguous and inconclusive manner. In this respect, though not only in this respect, ambiguity marks the writing of the leading radical historian of American diplomacy and the father of post-war revisionism. In William Appelman Williams' now classic study, *The Tragedy of American Diplomacy*, the reader is never quite clear—because Williams is never quite clear—whether America's institutions necessitated expansion or whether America has been expansionist out of the mistaken conviction that the continued well-being, if not the very existence, of these institutions required constant expansion. This ambiguity is particularly marked, both in the work of Williams and in the studies of other radical historians, when dealing with the earlier stages of America's world expansion.[1] Given the very limited char-

---

[1] "In the crisis of the 1890's," Williams writes, "when Americans *thought* that the continental frontier was gone, they advanced and accepted the argument that continued expansion in the face of overseas economic (and even territorial) empire provided the best, if not the only, way to sustain their freedom and prosperity." *The Tragedy of American Diplomacy*, p. 21. Was this "thought" correct or mistaken? Did it merely reflect the necessities imposed by America's economic institutions or did it create a "necessity" of its own? Williams will not say. Instead, he argues (pp. 45–47) that while overseas economic expansion was "important" to the national economy, the conviction of business groups that such expansion was crucial is, in the last analysis, all that maters and this even if the conviction was

acter of America's foreign economic involvement in these earlier stages, particularly in Asia, the radical historian, unwilling simply to equate capitalism with imperialism, is perforce driven to emphasize conviction. Even when applied to the much later period of World War II, the argument of necessity appears to have a *prima facie* implausibility when based upon America's *existing* foreign economic involvement. This is why conviction is still prominently stressed when explaining America's immediate post-war expansion, and why our expansion is still seen so largely in terms of what America's leaders presumably *believed* to be the needs of our institutions rather than simply the objective needs of those institutions.[2] This is also why many radical analyses emphasize that insofar as America's post-war anticommunism was based upon a Soviet threat to American interests it was a myth; but insofar as anticommunism was based upon a fear of what might happen to the domestic economy if we could not implement our expansionist goals it was real. Yet it makes a difference whether America's expansion is found to have resulted primarily from an institutional necessity or from a mistaken conviction about our institutional needs—and this even if convictions may prove as impervious to change as institutions.

quite mistaken. The importance of conviction—however mistaken—as an independent force is also emphasized in Walter LaFeber, *The New Empire: An Interpretation of American Expansion, 1860–1898* (1963).

[2] The idea that domestic welfare depended upon overseas economic activity, Williams writes, "is the crucial factor in understanding and interpreting American foreign policy in the 1930's—and in subsequent decades. Americans thought and believed that such expansion was essential, and their actions followed from that supposition." *Tragedy of American Diplomacy*, pp. 186–87.

It may of course be argued that conviction itself is essentially the reflection of a society's economic and social institutions and of the interests thereby generated. But if this view is accepted, to explain expansion in terms of conviction is, in effect, to explain expansion in terms of institutional structures and the needs presumably inherent in these structures. Moreover, if this view is once taken it makes very little sense to speak of mistaken conviction as a principal cause of action, save in the meaning that ideas, once generated, may then have a life of their own. It is difficult to believe that this is primarily what radical historians have in mind when stressing the role of conviction in America's world expansion. Practically the whole of American diplomacy since the turn of the century would then have to be understood in terms of intellectual error (for that is what the argument of mistaken conviction obviously means if taken seriously). Not only would this interpretation seem implausible on its face, it would resemble, while outdoing, the liberal-realist interpretation in the latter's emphasis on intellectual error as the great source of our difficulties in diplomacy. The only difference would be over the content of the error (and even this difference, as we shall presently see, may not prove as great as is commonly thought).

Indeed, an emphasis on mistaken conviction would appear almost nonsensical *if* it is assumed that men's ideas are essentially the reflection of a society's economic and social institutions and of the interests thereby generated. For even if it is true that ideas, once generated, may have a life of their own, this truth is scarcely applicable to the case at hand. The socio-economic institutions which presumably gave rise in the late nineteenth and early twentieth centuries to the conviction that we must pursue world expansion have not disappeared. To the contrary, these institutions have grown stronger in the course of the century, as the radical critic rightly insists. How, then, can the conviction that led to expansion be mistaken?[3]

Nor is this all. To the extent that the roots of expansion are traced to conviction, the nature of conviction itself may be less than apparent. Conviction may be established by action—that is, by the objective situation—in which case there is no need to rely more than incidentally upon what men presumably believed as evidenced by their words. But the significance of conviction as an explanation of action arises precisely because the meaning of action is itself unclear or because the reasons for which action is allegedly taken do not seem warranted by the objective circumstances attending the action. What was the nature of the conviction that prompted America's global expansion in this century? The response of radical historians who emphasize, in however ambiguous a manner, the significance of conviction is to insist upon identifying conviction with what American leaders presumably thought were the requirements of the economic system (hence the requirements of the political system as well). Yet there is no compelling reason for doing so unless this identification is first assumed. Given the variety of ration-

---

[3] It is another matter to argue that if expansion was not a necessity in an earlier period it has now become so, that the prosperity and cohesiveness of the American system as constituted today are dependent, and critically so, upon retaining control over an integrated Capitalist world order. But even if this argument is accepted, it still does not follow that there is any necessity for expansion inherent in America's institutional structures.

ales that have been made for American foreign policy, the highly selective procedure by which conviction is thus established in much radical history cannot but be suspect. For the method employed can hardly fail to "prove" what it sets out to prove. If the radical assumption is not made, however, there is no apparent reason for refusing to attribute conviction to still other considerations American statesmen have so regularly invoked in justifying their actions. No doubt, these other considerations—for example, security—may have been mistaken. But they cannot simply be dismissed out of hand because they were mistaken. If the conviction that America's economy required constant expansion abroad is accepted at face value as an explanation for action, though the conviction was mistaken, there is no apparent reason to dismiss the belief that America's security has required an expansionist policy, though this belief was also mistaken.

In this connection one sympathetic critic of the Williams school has noted: "Just as we do not accept Dean Rusk's public analysis of the causes of the Vietnam war, though recognizing the value of understanding why he believes what he does, so it would be foolish to simply accept, without further questioning, the rationale offered for their policies by the men of the late nineteenth century."[4] The point is well taken, though it is not quite correct to say that radical historians simply accept the rationale offered for their policies by the men of the late nineteenth century. What they accept is only that part of the rationale congenial to their interpretation. They do

[4] Marilyn B. Young, "American Expansion, 1870–1900: The Far East," in *Towards a New Past*, p. 179.

the same for subsequent periods of American diplomacy. Thus in the analysis of the origins of the cold war, radical critics almost invariably cite the testimony given by Assistant Secretary of State Dean Acheson in November, 1944, before a special Congressional Committee on Post-war Economic Policy and Planning. Williams appears to have been the first to cite this testimony and he believes that it casts "a dazzling light on American foreign policy ever since that date."[5]

The gist of Acheson's testimony was that America had to have foreign markets to absorb its "unlimited creative energy" if the nation were not to slide back into the depression of the pre-war years. The only alternative to foreign markets, Acheson declared, would be to consume what we produce, which would require that we "completely change our Constitution, our relations to property, human liberty, our very conceptions of law. And nobody contemplates that." To the radical historian, Acheson's statement clearly reveals the common conviction of America's corporate leaders. This may be true. It does not follow, however, that the statement also reveals the nerve root of American policy and the origins of the cold war. Why take this statement of Acheson's and not others which had a quite different emphasis, unless of course it is simply assumed that no other rationale can account for America's post-war policy? Indeed, why may we not argue that such statements as the one cited above obscure far more than they reveal the true sources of policy, that their purpose is largely to elicit support for a policy that is pursued primarily for quite different reasons? The argument

[5] *Tragedy of American Diplomacy*, p. 235.

may be false but it cannot be disposed of in the manner radical critics are wont to employ.

It would be unfair to say that these considerations are entirely ignored by radical historians who stress the importance of conviction. Although they may reject altogether the view that considerations of physical security can in any way explain American diplomacy in this century, they do not reject the view that there have been wellsprings of action other than the presumed needs of the American economy. Thus the commitment to the principle of self-determination is seen by some radical historians as having been something more than a merely verbal form.[6] Even when this commitment is found to have been betrayed in practice by the insistence that other peoples cannot solve their problems satisfactorily unless they imitate the American experience, there remains the question why we have so insistently sought to project, or impose, American values on the world. There is no compelling reason why this insistence may not be attributed to motives other than those identified with the presumed needs of American capitalism, unless of course it is simply taken for granted that no other motive can plausibly—or even possibly—account for a phenomenon as old as human history.

It is not even the case that radical historians reject the security motivation in accounting for America's expansion. They do insist that America's physical security has never been threatened in this century and that, in consequence, the fear of attack cannot have provided a plausible motivation for action. They do not reject the view that America's security in the

[6] Williams clearly sees it as something more than a merely verbal form, as does Levin in his *Woodrow Wilson and World Politics*.

greater than physical sense provides a plausible motivation. Indeed, most radical historians and critics
generally not only agree that security in this broader
sense provides a plausible motivation for policy but
insist that apprehension over the integrity and well-
being of America's institutions provides *the* explanation for our expansion. They differ mainly over
whether the apprehension has been well founded.
For those who believe that this apprehension has
been well founded, and never more so than today,
the problem of accounting for its persistence does not
arise. America's persistently expansionist and counterrevolutionary strategy is, on this view, solidly
rooted in self-interest, if not of the collective then of
the ruling class. But for those who believe it to have
been mistaken the problem clearly does arise. Why
have we so persistently identified America's welfare
and prosperity with a world that is, in Williams'
phrase, stabilized in a pro-American equilibrium?
Why have we believed that America's institutions
can only flourish, to employ the familiar euphemism
of American statesmen, in a congenial international
environment?

The broad response of the radical historian is, it
would appear, simply to restate the question in de-
claratory form. However mistaken the conviction
that America's security in the greater than physical
sense is dependent upon an ever-expanding American
system, this conviction is held to afford the essential
reason for America's expansionist—and counterrevolutionary—foreign policy. But this response does
not appear to differ markedly from a more conventional critique which also finds the explanation of
America's expansion (and certainly America's "globalism") largely in the conviction that the integrity

of the nation's institutions and the quality of its domestic life are dependent upon a world that, if not made over in the American image, at least remains "open" to our influence and example. The belief that America can only regenerate herself by regenerating the world, that the future of America's institutions can be assured only if they continue to provide the dominant model for the world, is part and parcel of a conventional critique. In emphasizing the importance of this belief as a source of America's expansion the radical critic says little that has not already been said.

If radical historiography has anything distinctive to contribute to this now familiar theme it must be found in the insistence that we have defined our security essentially in economic terms. What is distinctive to the radical critique is not the contention that we have interpreted our security in such a manner as to require—and justify—American predominance in the world, but the contention that this predominance has been sought principally in order to preserve and to strengthen capitalism at home. In turn, the preservation and strengthening of American capitalism has been seen to require the consolidation and extension of capitalism abroad. Thus the freedom we have sought to universalize above all other freedoms is freedom of enterprise; the institution we have provided as a model for others to follow above all other institutions is capitalism.

Here again, note must be made of the radical habit of emphasizing statements that appear to support this view of the nature of conviction and ignoring those that do not (or contending the latter merely obscure the true nature of policy). An example is provided by the Truman Doctrine. The Truman Doctrine did not commit the nation to saving the world for corporate capitalism. It did not identify freedom with capitalism. Nor did it declare that all freedom is dependent upon freedom of enterprise. There was no suggestion that the world should —or must—adopt the American system. The Truman Doctrine did not even suggest that the American system could survive only if it became a world system. It did declare that "nearly every nation must choose between alternative ways of life." But it defined these alternative ways—freedom and totalitarianism—almost entirely in libertarian and political terms. And it committed the United States to assisting "free people to work out their own destinies in their own way." Whatever else may be said of the Truman Doctrine, its words scarcely support the radical position. On the contrary, what is generally acknowledged to be the most significant postwar statement of American policy supports the view that freedom was not tied to capitalism let alone made dependent upon capitalism. This is why a radical critique either ignores the Truman Doctrine or insists that it obscures the true nature of America's objectives. But if it is argued that the Truman Doctrine obscures our true objectives, there is no apparent reason for not applying the argument to statements that in the radical view reveal those objectives.

By so defining the conviction that has equated security with the expansion of American power and influence, the radical critique must once again raise objections earlier raised against the methods by which the nature of conviction is established in radical historiography. Why must conviction be equated with the needs of the American economic system, unless this equation is first assumed? Why must it be assumed unless it is further assumed that no other motive can possibly account for a phenomenon as old as human history? But even if these objections are set aside, the distinctiveness of the conviction that, in the radical view, has prompted our expansion may be easily overdrawn. Although insistent upon the primacy of our commitment to capitalism abroad, and equally insistent upon attributing this commitment to our conviction about the needs of the domestic economic system, with few exceptions radical historians emphasizing the importance of conviction have not denied that liberal democratic political forms (which we have persisted in seeing as a corollary of self-determination) have also formed a part of our definition of a congenial world.[7] The triumph of liberal-capitalist internationalism may be seen as having been invariably equated with the economic and political interests of America as the principal guarantor and beneficiary of this order, but the triumph was nevertheless to be one of capitalism and liberal-democracy. This is the case even if American policy in this century is seen as little more than a commitment to a policy of the Open Door. Unless the Open Door is deliberately tailored to fit the claim that the radical critic has set out to prove, emphasis upon its significance for American diplomacy hardly establishes the radical contention respecting the nature of conviction—or, for that matter, of policy. The American insistence upon the Open Door, wherever this

[7] It is another matter to argue that this definition has been consistently subverted in practice, particularly since World War II by the support of repressive anti-liberal regimes in preference to the risk of change that might be taken over by the revolutionary left.

has been possible, has without doubt been an insistence upon a world receptive to America's economic expansion. It has also been an insistence upon a world receptive to America's political expansion. In its broadest and most significant sense, the Open Door has been in essence the claim of the great power to access—that is, the claim to control and to order its environment. To equate American policy with the Open Door is not to prove the radical contention that we have consistently defined our security primarily in economic terms. It is merely another way of stating this contention.[8]

Moreover, a conventional, though critical, historiography need not deny—and, for the most part, does not deny—that the congenial environment we have sought and have even deemed essential to our security in the broader sense has meant, among other things, a Capitalist environment. Nonradical critics may deny that we have made capitalism the centerpiece of our vision of world order and that we have seen all freedom as dependent upon freedom of enterprise. With few exceptions, they do not deny that we have seen capitalism as an integral part of a congenial international environment. (To the contrary, they have made the insistence that others adopt our institutions, economic institutions included, a focal point of criticism.) Certainly, it would be absurd to

---

[8] Williams writes that those "who dismissed the [Open Door] policy as irrelevant, misguided, or unsuccessful erred to two respects. They missed its deep roots in the American past and its importance at the time, and they failed to realize that the policy expressed the basic strategy and tactics of America's secular and imperial expansion in the twentieth century." *Tragedy*, p. 45. But the principal issue is not whether it is possible to find in the Open Door the basic strategy and tactics of America's expansion in this century. Instead, it is the meaning of the policy itself.

argue that we have been indifferent to whether our efforts promoted a Capitalist or a Socialist environment, only so long as it was democratic. That the Marshall Plan was designed to save the Capitalist economies of Western Europe, though this was by no means its only purpose, is therefore scarcely a radical revelation. That in helping to restore these economies we strengthened, and intended to strengthen, capitalism as a system of world power is equally apparent. Nor can it come as a surprise to be told that a major purpose of foreign aid has been to encourage that such development as does occur in underdeveloped states follows Capitalist ways and practices when this express purpose has been written into almost every foreign aid bill. No doubt, the radical critic is right in insisting that in our foreign aid we have sought to promote only such development as is firmly rooted in a Capitalist framework because this framework affords the best assurance of our continued freedom of access to raw materials and investments. It is equally clear, however, that still another reason is the fear that any other course of development, and certainly one that takes a strongly collectivist form, would mean that the American example was no longer relevant to much of the world. The prospect of the growing irrelevance of the American example must raise, in turn, the issue of American security in the greater than physical sense. At least it must do so if the proposition is once accepted that the integrity of the nation's institutions and the quality of its domestic life require a congenial international environment.

Given the circumstances in which it must be realized, the equation of American security with a congenial international environment has clearly required both an expansionist and a counterrevolutionary policy. The appreciation of this consequence, however, is surely not unique to a radical critique. Others have been almost equally insistent in pointing to the consequences of identifying world stability—in effect, the status quo—with American security. But the issue is not primarily one of identifying the consequences to which the equation of security and stability has led. It is rather the reasons or motives that have prompted the equation and that have made it so persistent. If the answer is not to be found in the objective forces generated by American capitalism, it must be sought in the variety of motives that have always led preponderant powers to identify their preponderance with their security and, above all, perhaps, in the fear arising simply from the loss of preponderance itself. The belief that the loss of preponderance must result in a threat to the well-being of the collective, and this irrespective of the material benefits preponderance confers, is so constant a characteristic of imperial states that it may almost be considered to form part of their natural history. That America, with its overweening sense of mission, should conform to this recurring pattern of response can occasion little surprise.[9]

[9] Robert Heilbroner calls our attention to the nature of the endemic fear evoked by the prospective loss of preponderance in his essay "Counter-revolutionary America," *Commentary* (April, 1967), pp. 31–38. ". . . There *is* a threat in the specter of a Communist or near-Communist supremacy in the underdeveloped world. It is that the rise of Communism would signal the end of capitalism as the dominant world order, and would force the acknowledgment that America no longer constituted the model on which the future of world civilization would be mainly based" (p. 37). It is, Heilbroner observes, "the fear of losing our place in the sun," and not the economic benefits conferred by preponderance, that prompts a counterrevolutionary policy.

69

It does not follow from these considerations that between radical and nonradical critiques the differences in the interpretation given to conviction are negligible. What does follow is that the differences between the two tend to become blurred and that, in consequence, it is difficult to see the distinctive qualities of the radical critique. If the radical critique is understood to mean that we have been expansionist out of mistaken conviction, that we have identified our need to expand with our security in the greater than physical sense, and that in expanding we have sought to universalize American values (while serving as principal guarantor and beneficiary of world order *à l'americaine*), then even if it granted that capitalism is the foremost of those values it is still not easy to see wherein the critique is sharply distinguished from a more conventional criticism.

* * *

We come back then to the point that has been emphasized from the outset of this essay. The distinctiveness of the radical left's critique must be found in the contention that America's foreign policy is essentially a response to the structural needs of American capitalism. If this contention is once abandoned, or seriously modified, differences will still remain between a radical and a more conventional criticism but these differences will no longer appear either profound or irreconcilable. Whatever the waverings and inconsistencies of particular radical critics, whatever the apparently independent role they may give to conviction and to interests that are not essentially rooted in the economic and social structure of American society, in the end it is only this contention that clearly sets them apart. No doubt, the radical position ought not to be pushed to the point of caricature, whether through a mechanical application of its essential contention or through the exclusion of other factors which are admitted to influence the nation's diplomacy. It is not denied that ideology may acquire a momentum of its own and, in the American case, has clearly done so. Even so, the question remains: What is central and what is peripheral to the radical analysis? The answer is not in real doubt. America's expansion—the drive to pacify and to integrate the global environment under American leadership and control—must be understood primarily as the outcome of forces generated by American capitalism.

Thus for all his ambiguity about the role of conviction, in the end Williams too is driven to the position that the roots of America's expansion must be found in the structural needs of an acquisitive, Capitalist society. He may interpret conviction as having re-enforced and aggravated this inherent propensity of American capitalism to expand. But unless we are to conclude that American diplomacy in this century has been little more than the result of mistaken conviction, we must conclude that this conviction, baneful as Williams finds it, is the inevitable consequence of an underlying and unchanging socio-economic reality. In the absence of a basic change in the institutional structure of American society, the essential character of the nation's foreign policy cannot be fundamentally altered. Enlightened statesmen—conservative statesmen, as it turns out—may temporize and even momentarily stay the inherently expansionist thrust of that policy. At best, however, a policy of the Open Door at home initiated by conservatives would be a holding operation. At the close of *The Tragedy of American Diplomacy*, Williams calls for an "enlightened conservatism" which can act upon the validity of the radical analysis by abandoning the conviction that America's well-being is dependent upon expansion. Yet he is at pains to emphasize that this is only a "short-run" solution, leaving the implication that expansion is, after all, rooted in America's institutions and that the abandonment of conviction, even if that were possible, is not enough.[10]

It needs to be emphasized that the view of Williams taken here is by no means the only possible one. It is possible to interpret him as saying that America's expansion has been throughout the result of mistaken conviction, despite the fact that this interpretation leads to curious and even nonsensical results. Williams almost encourages this interpretation by his insistence that America's intentions (and ideals) have been on the whole worthy but that they have been subverted by the general view (*weltanschauung*) America has entertained of itself and of the world which finds the nation's prosperity and freedom dependent upon an ever-expanding American system. This conflict within and between America's ideals and practice constitutes the essence of the persisting crisis in American diplomacy. In turn, the triumph in practice of the obsession to make the world over in the American image—that is, to dominate the world—defines the tragedy of American

---

[10] This implication is further supported, though again not without ambiguity, in Williams' essay *The Great Evasion: An Essay on the Contemporary Relevance of Karl Marx and on the Wisdom of Admitting the Heretic in the Dialogue about America's Future* (1964).

diplomacy. Yet the principal reason Williams offers for this inner conflict in which the nation has suppressed its "better self" is the mistaken "view" we have entertained of ourselves and of the world. Once again, then, we are back to an argument, the structure of which bears a remarkable affinity to the structure of the liberal-realist critique with its essential dichotomy of good intentions and unfortunate actions.[11]

In assessing the radical position, it is not enough to ask whether this position is plausible. The radical critic is not content with plausibility. Alternative interpretations, he argues, cannot possibly account for the expansionist character of American foreign policy in this century. Why not? Why may we not explain America's expansion in terms of the most apparent of historical experiences? Why may we not say simply that the interests of states expand roughly with their power and that America has been no exception to this experience? Certainly, radical critics do not admit to the belief that America is an exceptional nation which in expanding did a very unexceptional thing. On the other hand, we may safely dismiss the possibility that America is an unexceptional nation which has done as a world power some-

[11] Perhaps the key to these apparent incongruities is to be found in John Higham's appraisal (in reviewing Williams' *The Contours of American History*) that Williams "duplicates the Beardian combination of tough materialism with tender idealism, and has the same compulsion to discover a hidden core of virtue beneath the solid surface of American life"; *Studies on the Left* (vol. 2, 1961), pp. 74–75. If so (and the influence on Williams of Charles Beard's analysis in *The Idea of National Interest* and *The Open Door at Home* is apparent), Williams also duplicates much of the Beardian confusion and obscurantism. And this may be said without in the least detracting from the significance of Williams' impressive achievements.

thing other world powers before her have not done. Why, then, is the radical explanation necessary in order to account for America's expansion *per se*?

Of course, one may go further and ask: Why does interest expand with power? But even if the radical critic does insist upon raising this question, to do so can scarcely advance his argument. Whatever the reasons that may account for what appears to be a near universal experience, these reasons can scarcely be employed in support of the radical argument. The radical view is intent upon showing that America's expansion must be explained essentially in terms of our social structure, whereas the rough correspondence that appears almost invariably to obtain between power and interests must evidently be explained independently of the particular social structure of states.

Is it possible, however, to understand the radical critics as arguing, despite their insistence to the contrary, that America is exceptional in its aggressiveness and in its insatiable urge to dominate? If this is their meaning, then it is difficult to argue further that the explanation of these exceptional characteristics is to be found in capitalism. At the very least, it must be argued that these characteristics have their source in a distinctively American version of capitalism. But this is only another way of saying that America's persistent expansiveness and aggressiveness are not to be found so much in capitalism as in other factors, which when combined with capitalism produce such unfortunate consequences. (May not one of these factors be an overweening sense of mission, the roots of which can scarcely be traced to capitalism? May not another factor be the very magnitude of American power, particularly since World War II? And, if so, does this not support a view about the nature of power, not Capitalistic power but any power?)

Confronted by these obvious considerations, radical critics may fall back upon an argument against which no response appears to be of any avail. By definition, the possibility is ruled out that a Capitalist state can pursue any policy other than an expansionist one, just as by definition the possibility is ruled out that a truly Socialist state *would* pursue an expansionist policy. This being so, there is no need to consider whether other factors may plausibly, or even possibly, account for the expansion of American power. By definition, this expansion can have no other explanation. In the words of one radical critic, "imperialism is capitalism which has burst the boundaries of the nation state . . . [The] two phenomena are inseparable: there can be no end to imperialism without an end to capitalism and to capitalist relations of production."[12]

Against this familiar metaphysic it is as futile to cite the history of imperialism before capitalism as it is to cite the imperialism of those who presumably herald the coming of the post-Capitalist, hence post-imperialist, era. If imperialism existed before capitalism, as it evidently did, this is explained in terms of an economic necessity that capitalism (together with technology) has enabled men to transcend, although unable itself to transcend imperialism. If ostensibly Socialist states resort to expansionist foreign policies, this is explained by the fact that they are not—or are no longer—truly Socialist

[12] David Horowitz, *Empire and Revolution: A Radical Interpretation of Contemporary History* (1969), p. 38.

75

states, or by the fact that in a still predominantly Capitalist world no Socialist state is free to realize its true nature. Thus the expansion of the Soviet Union at the close of World War II has been explained by the necessities imposed upon a Socialist state that must secure its existence in a Capitalist world. The explanation wore increasingly thin as Soviet power grew but Soviet determination not to relinquish control over Eastern Europe remained unchanged. It became threadbare in 1968 with the Soviet intervention in Czechoslovakia, whereupon many reached the conclusion that the Soviet Union was no longer a truly Socialist state. (To some, the Soviet Union, in contrast to China, had become increasingly bureaucratic. Moreover, it had become, relative to China and other undeveloped states, affluent. That undeveloped societies could not become equally bureaucratic is simply assumed. That the Soviet Union's relative affluence somehow altered what had formerly been Socialist behavior remains inexplicable, unless it is assumed that wealth is somehow incompatible with socialism—an assumption otherwise at odds with radical assumptions about the domestic preconditions of socialism.) Like true love for the philosopher who holds it incompatible with any intrusion of the claims of the ego, true socialism for the radical believer is held incompatible with the control or domination of others. Reality, therefore, proves nothing about either love or socialism. It also proves nothing about capitalism. Thus it is futile to argue that when imperialism has been undertaken by Capitalist states its costs have often outweighed its benefits to the collective. This argument only prompts the response: Who pays for imperialism? To show that Capitalists may themselves pay on occasion, as in Vietnam, merely proves that the psychological certainty required by capitalism (for access to and control over sources of raw materials, for continued freedom to invest) may in turn require temporary sacrifices.

Clearly, this method of argumentation will not do. If the radical critic is to establish his case, he cannot do so by falling back upon a metaphysic about the nature of capitalism and its needs. Nor can he simply ignore alternative interpretations of America's expansion, and particularly one that accounts for this expansion—if only in a very general way—without resorting to problemmatic assumptions about the effects of social structure upon state behavior. The objection may of course be raised that even if a rough correspondence between power and interest does appear as a near universal experience, it is precisely because an interpretation of expansion based upon this experience is so general that its utility as applied to a specific case or even an historical type of expansion can be disregarded. A radical economist in a widely read recent analysis of American imperialism dismisses the attempt to explain imperialism "as a multifarious response to a common opportunity that consists simply in disparity of power" by noting: "This interpretation, correct or incorrect, is at so high a level of abstraction that it contributes nothing to an understanding of historical differences in types and purposes of aggression and expansion. It is entirely irrelevant, for example, to an explanation of the historical expansion of capitalist society into a world system, or of why this expansion is associated with a growing disparity of power between a few nations that are exceptionally rich and many nations that are continuously poor."[13] That a general interpretation of expansion may contribute little to an understanding of historical differences in types of expansion is no doubt true. It does not follow, however, that general explanations are therefore irrelevant. All that follows is that specific cases cannot be understood in their specificity merely by applying to them otherwise valid general explanations.

Moreover, the radical critic is scarcely in a position to reject an interpretation of expansion simply because it is at a "high level of abstraction." Whatever else may be said of the radical interpretation —whether it be Leninist, a subsequent variation thereof, or even Maoist—it has never suffered from modesty in claim. Nor are occasional radical disclaimers to the contrary persuasive. The same critic, quoted above, who rejects an interpretation of expansion because it is at so high a level of abstraction is not for this reason inhibited from doing himself what he condemns when done by others. It is true that Magdoff warns perfunctorily against an oversimplified " 'pure' economic imperialism formula. The search for unadulterated economic motives of foreign policy decisions will serve as a useful hypothesis in a large number of cases. But it will fail if one expects to find such for *each and every* act of political and military policy."[14] There is surely a huge difference, however, between an interpretation that "contributes nothing to an understanding in types and purposes of aggression and expansion" and one that merely fails to explain *"each and every*

[13] Harry Magdoff, *The Age of Imperialism: The Economics of U.S. Foreign Policy* (1969), p. 13.
[14] *Ibid.*

act of political and military policy." Apparently the latter interpretation, despite its admitted generality, does permit us to understand specific cases, even in their specificity. It only fails if we expect it to account for each and every specific act.

Magdoff does not explain to what we are to attribute this remarkable power of explanation. Nor, for that matter, does he resist attempting to explain *each and every* act of American foreign policy in terms of the nature of capitalism and its needs. Indeed, he no sooner explicitly disavows the "pure economic imperialism formula" than he implicitly endorses it, and through an argument ostensibly designed to show why it does not work. Governments can spend billions to dominate a country "even though the resulting control protects profits in the millions for only one or two corporations. But the reality of imperialism goes far beyond the immediate purpose of this or that investor: the underlying purpose is nothing less than keeping as much as possible of the world open for trade and investment by the giant multilateral corporations."[15] Hence it makes no sense to explain isolated acts of policy in "bookkeeping" terms. And it makes no sense, Magdoff argues, because what is important is the retention of control over, or the possibility of access to, entire areas. But what is this argument designed to establish, if we set aside the interest of this or that investor, other than the very point Magdoff sets out to deny: that government policy is based on strict cost-accounting rules. What presumably distinguishes government cost accounting is that it must be placed, if it is to be

---

[15] *Ibid.*, p. 14. For the same argument, see Paul A. Baran and Paul M. Sweezy, "Notes on a Theory of Imperialism," *Monthly Review* (March, 1966), p. 16.

properly understood, in a very broad context. The cost-accounting argument does not detract from the "pure economic imperialism formula." On the contrary, it is used to support the formula.

Of course, this cannot be the last word. Even when considered in a broad context, the cost-accounting argument may, and does, break down as an explanation of policy. If *each and every* act is to be explained, other and higher grounds must be chosen. What is decisive to capitalism, Magdoff writes in a passage that sums up a whole literature, *"is that the option of foreign investment (and foreign trade) should remain available.* For this to be meaningful, the business system requires, as a minimum, that the political and economic principles of capitalism should prevail and that the door be fully open for foreign capital at all times . . . . How much or how little an open door may be exploited at any given time is not the issue. The *principle* must be maintained. . . ."[16] But we must ask why? Why must the option remain open, the principle maintained, if the costs exceed the benefits (and this however broad the context in which costs-benefits are calculated)? Are we not finally driven back, though by a different route, to the same metaphysic respecting the nature of capitalism and its needs?

Even if we take to heart, as we must, the stricture that specific cases of expansion cannot be understood in their specificity merely by applying to them otherwise valid general explanations, does the radical critique provide us with a novel understanding of the methods that have characterized America's expansion? It would not appear so. Although much has

[16] *Ibid.*, p. 20.

been made of the methods of expansion identified with the Open Door, a conventional historiography has also recognized in these methods the characteristic features of American expansion. In this respect, what distinguishes much of radical historiography is not its discovery of the methods identified with the Open Door, but its insistence upon the distinctiveness of these methods. Yet it is a surprisingly parochial view that finds in the Open Door a distinctively American contribution to the history of state expansion.[17] Clearly, the methods characterizing the Open Door policy have been especially suited to a nation that has enjoyed an economic preponderance and, at the same time, has prided itself in its anti-imperial commitment. The point remains that the method of indirect and informal empire is not an American invention. It is not even a Capitalist invention.

At any rate, an emphasis upon the methods of America's expansion does not, and cannot, distinguish the radical critique. It is in the purposes or ends of the Open Door, and not its methods, that this critique marks a sharp break from other criticism. The ends of the Open Door are deduced from what the radical critic invariably assumes to be the root sources of America's expansion. We return then to the question earlier raised: Is the radical interpretation of America's expansion *per se* a necessary one? Unless we are to fall back upon a metaphysic about the nature of capitalism and its needs, the answer must be that it is not.

If the radical explanation of America's expansion is not a necessary one, as a specific contribution to

[17] As does the Williams school. For a needed and useful corrective to this view, cf. Ernest R. May, *American Imperialism: A Speculative Essay* (1968).

the understanding of an historical case of expansion, is it at least as plausible as alternative explanations? Even if we assume the validity of a general interpretation which shows expansion as ultimately independent of the particular social structure of states, there remains the possibility that in a specific instance—or even type—of expansion social structure will prove to be the dominant cause. At issue here is not a dogma about capitalism and its inherent nature but an explanation of the effects of American capitalism upon America's expansion. Is it plausible to assume that America's expansion was essentially a response to the structural needs of American capitalism rather than to the dynamics of state competition or the search for a security the expansive dimensions of which have been largely determined by a tradition of geographical detachment and a distinctive sense of mission? Whatever answer one may give to this question, it must not be confused with the position that we have sought a congenial international environment which would reflect or prove receptive to our institutional forms, which we could largely direct and control, and from which we would derive benefits—not least of all economic. For this position, though it may be readily conceded, amounts to little more than the assertion that we have behaved in much the same manner and for much the same reasons great powers have always behaved. The recognition of this similarity may be a worthy correction to an uncritical view of American diplomacy, but it has little, if any, bearing on the question posed here.

*　　*　　*

The preceding considerations must be kept in mind when examining the radical interpretation of the origins of the cold war and of subsequent American diplomacy. It is the period beginning with World War II that provides the principal grist for the radical mill and, one is driven to conclude, the only real grist. Indeed, a close reading of radical history itself appears to bear out this conclusion. Radical historians do not deny that World War II marks a significant change in the tactics and intensity of commitment to the expansionist strategy America has presumably pursued throughout the century. Nor do they deny that the war marks the first time this strategy is consistently and effectively implemented on a global scale. Given these changes, however, what remains to the radical claim of a striking continuity in American diplomacy other than the broad insistence that our *aspiration* throughout has been to achieve a stable liberal-capitalist world order under American leadership? Even if this continuity in grand design is admitted, what is its practical significance if the means of policy, the determination to achieve the ends of policy, and the very scope given these ends have all greatly changed?

Continuities are of course always possible to find, provided one looks hard enough and exercises sufficient care in definition. The question remains whether the result of the effort is more to obscure significant differences than to illuminate meaningful continuities. It is only by downgrading the all-important issue of means, by slighting the degree of determination shown in the pursuit of ends, and by assuming that the nature of ends invariably determines their scope that radical historians can find a striking continuity between America's pre World War II and post World War II diplomacy, and thereby dismiss American isolationism in the interwar period as a myth conjured up by a conventional historiography. Of what, however, does this myth consist? It is no part of a conventional historiography to contend that the inter-war variant of isolationism meant a complete withdrawal from the world outside the Western Hemisphere. America's isolationism was never given either a commercial or an ideological expression and a conventional historiography has never contended otherwise. It is acknowledged that the inter-war years marked a steady, if unspectacular, expansion of America's interests, particularly America's economic interests. This expansion, with its evident bias in favor of stability and the status quo, was supported, though with widely varying effectiveness, by America's growing economic power. Within the hemisphere, American interests were occasionally supported by military power as well, though only in the area of the Caribbean and Central America. None of these points impairs the judgment that, on the whole, America continued to pursue an isolationist policy. What isolationism signified was no more and no less than the refusal to guarantee the post World War I status quo in Europe and Asia against change by force of arms. The issue of America's isolationism is not primarily one of determining what America's interests were in the post-war order, as radical critics assert. It is one of determining what commitments America was prepared to undertake to preserve those interests, however they are defined. And on this critical issue, at least, there is scarcely much room for argument.

If radical historians nonetheless reject America's inter-war isolationism as a myth, it is because of their insistence that American leaders sought throughout to preserve an international environment receptive to the nation's economic and political expansion. Even if this argument is accepted, and there is no apparent reason for rejecting it, the point remains that the means successive administrations were prepared to employ in order to preserve an environment congenial to American interests were strictly circumscribed. These limits on American power, as radical critics themselves acknowledge, resulted in the breakdown of the Open Door strategy once the revisionist states—notably Germany and Japan—decided to challenge this strategy by force of arms. Even in the radical view, then, American policy in the inter-war period is characterized by a growing disproportion between interest and power. In the conventional view, this disproportion is one of power to interest, in the sense that the power we would not employ was disproportionate to the interests we should have consistently and effectively pursued. In the radical view as well, however, there is a disproportion of power to interest, though the power we would not employ is considered disproportionate to interests we should never have pursued. At root here are markedly contrasting judgments on the nature and desirability of America's interests. But this disparity of judgment does not affect the common recognition of the limits placed on American power. So long as the limits on means persisted the question also persists whether the strategy of the Open Door was more an aspiration than a reality. Is it meaningful to speak of a policy when the requisite means of policy are nevertheless foresworn?

In the end, of course, America did forcibly intervene against the Axis Powers. In this fact the radical finds the final validation of his view that America's inter-war isolationism was always a myth. But the fact that America did ultimately intervene in Europe and Asia proves only what needs no proof : that a policy of refusing to undertake political-military commitments outside the hemisphere had to be abandoned once it became apparent that its continued pursuit threatened the loss of interests deemed vital. At the same time, the fact of intervention itself proves very little about the nature of those interests. Certainly, it does not prove that the compelling reason for intervening must be found in the unwillingness to abandon the strategy and goals of the Open Door rather than the fear that a Eurasia controlled by hostile powers would ultimately pose a threat to America's physical security. Even less does it prove that a Eurasia controlled by hostile powers would not have posed a threat to America's security in its greater than physical dimension.

What the radical insistence on viewing American intervention in terms of the Open Door does prove, if proof were needed, is simply that our domestic well-being, hence our security in the greater than physical sense, has been defined very largely in terms of an international order receptive to American institutions and interests. An Axis victory held out the promise of a world hostile to these institutions and interests, a world in which America's economic and political frontiers might have to become coextensive with its territorial frontiers, and thus a world in which prosperity and democracy in America itself might be gravely imperiled. The issue of physical security apart, it was clearly to prevent this threat from materializing that the decision was made to intervene. Radical historians do not dissent from this analysis. Instead, they emphasize that the threat followed from the manner in which American leaders

86

had traditionally defined the integrity and well-being of America's institutions, hence the manner in which they had traditionally defined America's security in its greater than physical dimension. This is no doubt the case. It does not follow, however, that in the circumstances in which it was applied the definition was mistaken and that the projected consequences to this country of an Axis victory could have been avoided if only American policy had not been committed to the expansionist goals of the Open Door. Nor do radical historians seriously contend—let alone demonstrate—otherwise.

For these reasons the radical treatment of the inter-war period lacks persuasiveness. The stress on continuity appears forced, unless it is kept to the level of grand design. At that level, it is largely dependent on speculative considerations that deal at least as much with motivation as with behavior. The result is to identify as policy what is often little more than aspiration. Moreover, a number of the examples that are offered from an earlier period seem labored when employed, as they invariably are employed, to establish a profound continuity with the present. The lengths to which the search for continuity are carried may be seen in the insistence on finding in yesterday's interventions in the Caribbean the microcosm of today's intervention in Vietnam. Yet to see in these disparate acts of intervention the consistent workings of an unchanging policy is possible only by obscuring differences that are crucial both to the conduct and understanding of statecraft. (One difference is that yesterday's interventions in the Caribbean *were* a microcosm. They expressed a traditional claim to a limited sphere of influence. It is scarcely possible to say the same for the intervention in Vietnam.)

Does the radical critique fare better when applied to the period beginning with World War II? As we have already noted, in radical historiography the war is considered significant in that it marks a change in the tactics and intensity of commitment to the expansionist strategy of the Open Door, though it does not mark a substantive change in the strategy itself. In the circumstances attending and following the war, that strategy, with its overriding aim of establishing a stable liberal-capitalist world order under American leadership and control, made conflict with the Soviet Union, and eventually with much of the remaining world, inevitable.

There are variations on this major theme, though the differences they reflect seem less significant than the similarities they affirm. Thus it is occasionally argued that American policy in the immediate postwar period must be explained primarily by the need to create a threat justifying cold war mobilization. On this view, the Soviet Union became the mortal enemy not so much because it posed an obstacle to our hegemonial strategy but because its existence served to sanction what was initially a domestic cure for the ills of American capitalism. It is only in a later phase of the cold war that a cure for these ills is increasingly sought abroad. But whether the cold war is held to have initially arisen from the commitment to an expansionist policy or from the need to create domestic support for a militarized economy, or from the two in equal proportion, is less important than the common conviction that the roots of the cold war must be found in the structural needs of American capitalism. Moreover, those who stress the initial commitment to a hegemonial strategy do not deny that this strategy required a militarized economy, just as those who stress the initial emphasis on a militarized economy do not deny that this strategy required a militarized politics. In either analysis, the Soviet Union had to become the enemy. In both, the threat posed by the Soviet Union was a myth.

The radical interpretation of the cold war thus neglects the structural causes of the conflict. On occasion, it is true, radical critics do acknowledge that the cold war initially resulted from a situation for which neither party can be held responsible. In this more sophisticated version, it is conceded that the real issue is not which side started the cold war but which side is responsible for the way in which the conflict developed and the lengths to which it was carried.[18] The concession is at best a limited one, however, usually made in passing and then only reluctantly. It could scarcely be otherwise, since an emphasis on the importance of the structural or systemic causes of the cold war must seriously detract from the central thrust of the argument. Yet no plausible account of Soviet-American hostility can neglect to emphasize the significance of the structural causes of this hostility. What had been prior to the war the center of the international system had suddenly collapsed. By destroying the pre-war balance of power —by creating a vacuum in the heart of Europe—the war resulted in a situation that could not but give rise to Soviet-American hostility. In the past, similar circumstances had invariably led to rivalry, often in-

[18] Cf. Williams, *The Tragedy of American Diplomacy*, pp. 206–207. Also, Lloyd C. Gardner, *Architects of Illusion: Men and Ideas in American Foreign Policy, 1941–1949* (1970), p. x.

tense, even between states that understood each other because they possessed many similarities of outlook and shared a common diplomatic tradition. Given this history, and given the fact that the cold war arose between states that did not understand each other, that entertained markedly divergent outlooks and shared no common diplomatic tradition, it seems evidently implausible to assume that conflict—even quite intense conflict—could have been avoided had one of the parties not been determined to pursue an expansionist policy.

If the radical interpretation is implausible in its neglect of the structural causes of the cold war, it does provide a needed corrective to the conventional portrayal of the American view of the post-war world (and hence the portrayal of American aims in the post-war world). It is the contention of conventional historiography—whether old or new—that the origins of the cold war must in part be understood in terms of two very different views of how the post-war world was to be organized: the universalist and the spheres-of-influence view. Whereas the Soviet Union was the champion of spheres of influence, the United States was presumably committed to the view that "all nations shared a common interest in all the affairs of the world" and that "national security would be guaranteed by an international organization."[19]

The radical critic is surely right in insisting that there is little in this description of the universalist view that corresponds to American policy during the period in question. Clearly, America's universalism

[19] Arthur Schlesinger, Jr., "Origins of the Cold War," *Foreign Affairs* (October, 1967), p. 26.

did not mean an opposition to any and all spheres of influence, for that opposition was betrayed by our continued claim to a sphere of influence in the Western Hemisphere and, beyond the hemisphere, to what was tantamount to a similar claim in the western Pacific. Nor can America's universalism be interpreted to mean the commitment to multilateralism as a method for safeguarding American interests. It is vain to point to the United Nations Charter, and to American support of the charter, as evidence of this commitment. The charter did not commit the great powers to multilateralism as a means for guaranteeing their interests. The charter's design of order was made dependent on the condition that the great powers would retain a basic identity of interests. It did not deal with the only contingency that could seriously threaten the vital interests of a great power but merely assumed that in this contingency—conflict between the great powers—each would seek to protect its interests in its own way and that the security system of the charter would become inoperative.

This was clearly the American understanding of the charter. Rather than to interpret our support of the United Nations as representing a serious commitment to multilateralism, this support should be seen as reflecting the belief, or hope, that the organization could be employed as a modest means for more effectively consolidating America's leadership in the post-war world. (The same may be said of the international economic institutions, predominantly of American inspiration, that were to emerge from the war.) In joining the United Nations America retained, and insisted on retaining, substantially the same freedom of action it had enjoyed in the past.

A tradition of unilateralism remained very nearly intact even after the decision was made to undertake formal territorial commitments outside the hemisphere. Given America's vast power and the weakness of her allies, not only were America's commitments for all practical purposes unilateral in character but so were her relations generally.

What, then, did America's universalism mean—above all, with respect to the Soviet Union? It evidently meant that we were opposed to certain kinds of spheres of influence, precisely the kind the Russians were establishing in Eastern Europe. But what did it mean in terms of a Soviet policy that would not have incurred our hostility? It will not do to answer that the question itself is meaningless. Even if it is granted that the Russians were compelled to pursue the policy they did in fact pursue, given the outlook and character of the Soviet regime, the question remains relevant unless it is assumed that the American outlook and character gave rise to no "compulsions" for American policy. More pointedly, what policy might the Russians have followed in the circumstances of the immediate post-war years, without arousing American opposition, that would have given them a degree of security at least roughly comparable to that enjoyed by the United States, while leaving that security in Russian hands (for that exclusive control was no more than America claimed and enjoyed)? It is, in fact, very difficult to imagine what that policy might have been. If this is so, it is difficult to avoid the conclusion that the only policy the Russians could have pursued which would not have incurred American hostility was one that placed Russian security—and not only security—largely at the mercy of the good intentions of others, above all,

America. There is no reason for assuming that America would have accepted such an arrangement in her own case. Why should it have appeared unreasonable and threatening that the Soviets refused a similar arrangement?

To the radical critic, the answer is clear. America's universalism was little more than a euphemism for an outlook and policy which sought to establish American supremacy in the post-war world. A policy intent upon making the world itself into an American sphere of influence is of necessity universalist in aim, just as it is of necessity opposed to spheres of influence from which its power and influence are excluded. If the radical response is overdrawn, if it fails to acknowledge the security motive that entered into American policy, it nevertheless contains a core of truth. Yet it is only by juxtaposition with an orthodox historiography that this response appears startling. What state that achieved the power and eminence America achieved by the end of World War II has not wanted and sought to have the world evolve in an equilibrium favorable to it? In America's case, a favorable equilibrium was evidently one that comprised the strengthening of capitalism. It is equally apparent that the strengthening of capitalism as a world system was seen as synonymous with the strengthening of American capitalism, the latter requiring the removal of the pre-war obstacles to American exports and investments while ensuring American access to needed raw materials. There is no reason to deny the radical claim that the world America sought to achieve in the post-war period, and from which America could only derive maximum advantage in view of her dominant economic and political position, was the familiar one of the Open Door.

At least there is no reason to deny this claim, provided the Open Door is given a sufficiently broad interpretation. To this extent, the interpretation of America's wartime diplomacy by Williams or, for that matter, by Kolko is unexceptionable. Thus it is scarcely a revelation to be told, as Kolko tells us, that "America's economic war aim was to save capitalism at home and abroad."[20] Surely, no one argues that our economic war aim was to promote socialism. It is another matter to argue, as Kolko does argue, that America's "core objectives were economic" and that "politics was only the instrument for preserving and expanding America's unprecedented power and position in the European and world economy."[21] The argument cannot rest simply upon an economic determinism which takes for granted what needs to be proved. What is the proof radical historians offer, apart from the careful selection of statements by American statesmen—a selection that is subject to those objections we have already raised? In Kolko's case it appears to consist largely in the fact, which no one disputes, that America's economic aims for the post-war world—and above all the aim of lowering the barriers to free trade—crystallized well ahead of her political aims. But this fact hardly bears out the major thesis that America's economic aims were all determining. Instead it indicates only that there was a widespread consensus over America's economic interests abroad, hence a widespread consensus over the kind of reconstructed world economy

[20] *The Politics of War*, p. 252.
[21] *Ibid.*

we would support in the post-war period, whereas a similar consensus did not exist with respect to political interests (or, at the very least, did not exist with respect to the means we would commit ourselves to, if necessary, in order to vindicate acknowledged interests). All this is understandable in the light of the American diplomatic experience. It proves nothing about the nature of America's core objectives.

Much of the opposition to a claim that might otherwise seem unexceptionable may be attributed to the assumption that to concede this claim is to concede still more specific claims. But it does not follow that if American leaders sought a world that would evolve in a pro-American equilibrium, they were also willing to employ any and all methods to achieve this goal—and did in fact employ them. The issue is one of historical evidence, not of logical deduction. If the evidence does support the contention that we sought, however ineffectively, to exploit our economic strength and Russia's economic need to the end of making Russia more tractable in Europe, it does not support the contention that we seriously tried to use America's atomic monopoly for the same end. Indeed, even if American leaders in 1945–46 had been intent on pursuing a policy that went beyond diplomatic protest and economic inducement, and even if the American public had been willing to support such a policy, there would probably have been no need to rely upon the atomic bomb. But the intent was not there, and even if it had been, it would not have elicited public support. Instead, the time-honored methods of American diplomacy were employed, with almost entirely negative results.

That our efforts did result in failure is not disputed by radical critics. The question the radical critique raises, however, is why did these efforts fail? If we were so intent on having our way in Eastern Europe, why did the advantages we presumably held count for so little in the end? The radical critique is content simply to register the fact of failure. But this scarcely seems adequate once we accept the thesis of a preponderant America determined to establish its hegemony in the post-war world and willing to employ the means necessary to achieve this goal. Given the failure of American policy in Eastern Europe, we can only conclude either that America's power did not confer a decisive advantage, that it was not sufficiently preponderant, or that American leaders were unwilling (or, in view of public opinion, unable) to exploit their advantage to the hilt. Of the two possible explanations, the latter is the more important—at least for the very early post-war period. It places in perspective the unending dispute over the significance of the atomic bomb in America's post-war diplomacy. Without doubt, possession of the bomb significantly contributed to the hardening of the American position on Eastern Europe and encouraged the expectation that this position would finally prevail. There is no evidence, however, that the bomb was ever explicitly used as a threat to moderate the Soviet position in Eastern Europe. Was the threat nevertheless implicit? Clearly it was in the sense that the United States could be expected to use the bomb in the event Soviet-American differences were to lead to war. But this suggests that possession of the bomb could prove no more effective in furthering American aims in Eastern Europe than the prospect that America would go to war, if necessary, to realize those aims. Radical critics do not argue that this prospect was ever a meaningful one. If not, the threat held out by possession of the atomic bomb was never meaningful as a means of dislodging the Soviets from a position already held.

The essence of the radical case, however, does not concern the means American leaders were allegedly intent upon employing to establish American supremacy in the post-war world. It is rather that in view of the limited aims of Soviet policy in Europe and, still more important, the vast superiority of power America enjoyed at the end of the war and in the years immediately thereafter, this nation had no security problem. Given this power preponderance, America was in a position to explore alternatives and even to make concessions that the Soviet Union, from its relatively weak and still insecure position, was not. In refusing to do so, in undertaking instead a course of action that crystallized the cold war, America was simply acting consistently with the premises of her expansionist strategy.

The radical reconstruction of the origins of the cold war thus rests on two central propositions: that American policy forced the Soviets to alter what were initially limited aims in Eastern Europe, and confined to Eastern Europe; and that in view of America's preponderant position of power considerations of security cannot plausibly account for this policy. Of the two propositions, the first necessarily remains the more conjectural. We do not know today, as American leaders did not know at the time, what the aims of the Soviets initially were in Eastern Europe. That the Soviets defined those aims in modest terms to their allies during the war proves nothing since it was in their interest to do so. That Soviet behavior in Eastern Europe initially appeared to bear out this limited definition, though even then

97

only in varying degree, may be explained by the desire to avoid arousing, so far as this was possible, Western fear and hostility. That the Soviets came to exercise complete control over Eastern Europe only after the cold war had clearly crystallized may only indicate that it was no longer necessary to observe the prudential restraints of an earlier period (and also that in view of the example set by Yugoslavia in 1948 the restraints of an earlier period could no longer be safely observed).

These considerations apart, it is surely reasonable to contend that American policy from early 1945 on could have no other result than to heighten Soviet apprehensions that their principal wartime ally sought to deny them a sphere of influence in Eastern Europe. Is it plausible to contend, however, that this was the principal, if not the only, reason for the eventual assertion of a sphere of domination in place of a moderate sphere of influence? In support of this contention, it is argued that so long as Russian security objectives were met the Soviets were willing to permit considerable internal freedom in Eastern Europe. But the argument only begs the question: what were those security objectives and how could they be satisfied? To answer that they were limited assumes that the outlook of the Soviet regime, the political psychology of its rulers, and the circumstances in which power was exercised, had no substantial effects on the manner in which the Soviet Union defined its security requirements. If that assumption cannot bear critical examination, neither can the argument that it was only Soviet apprehensions over their external security in the face of Western hostility that drove them to assert complete control over Eastern Europe. A generation later, in 1968, the Soviet position in Europe and in the world at large had changed and changed radically. Yet despite this change in the Soviet Union's world power position, despite the fact of Soviet control over Eastern Europe for more than two decades, despite the changes that had occurred within the Soviet Union, and despite the now almost complete passivity of America, Soviet leaders concluded that in the case of Czechoslovakia they still could not risk making the distinction between a sphere of influence and one of domination. Is it unreasonable to conclude that, in large measure, they could not do so now for the same reason they could not do so in an earlier period: the fear that the twin virus of liberalization and national independence might spread to the Soviet Union, threatening the structure of Soviet power and the very integrity of the Soviet state?

It may be argued that to the extent this fear prompted the Czech intervention it only serves to strengthen the view that Soviet control over Eastern Europe has been based throughout on considerations of security. But if this argument is granted, it must also be acknowledged that Soviet security needs are indeed distinctive and that this distinctiveness explains why the Soviets have been driven to equate a sphere of influence with one of domination. These considerations do not affect the further argument that the United States would have opposed a Soviet sphere of influence in Eastern Europe even if exercised in a manner more moderate than was in fact the case. This argument is probably well taken, though the question remains whether the nature of the opposition would have been the same.

It is another matter to argue that whatever the nature of Soviet aims in Eastern Europe, these aims did not extend beyond Eastern Europe. But no one knew, or could know, the extent of Soviet aims in Europe, whether at the close of the war or in the years immediately following the war. It is altogether possible that the Russians themselves did not know, in any immediate policy sense, and that they adjusted their aims according to circumstance and opportunity. Even assuming that the Russians never seriously contemplated expanding into Western Europe by conventional military means, conditions in Western Europe after 1946 appeared to hold out ample opportunities for expansion by other means. One need not subscribe to the position that ideology and the circumstances in which he exercised power compelled Stalin to constant expansion in order to argue that Western Europe's weakness and instability nevertheless provided the temptation to expand through indirect means. In comparable circumstances, most great states have sought to expand, particularly when they could do so without serious risk of war. Why is it assumed that the Soviets, whose hostility toward and fear of the West were not in doubt, never entertained expansionist aims beyond Eastern Europe, so long as such further expansion could be undertaken without serious risk of war?

From the vantage point of the late 1960s, Gabriel Kolko[22] dismisses the wartime apprehensions of the United States and Great Britain that the Soviet Union might attempt to employ the Communist parties of Western Europe as the means for expanding Soviet power over the continent. Instead, Kolko argues, the Soviet Union, pursuing a "conservative" policy, exercised a restraining influence on the forces of the

[22] *The Politics of War.*

left. In doing so, the Soviet Union may have been decisive in salvaging the pre-war status quo. "If the Russians had not given the West a respite, in fact Washington may have realized its fears everywhere in 1945. For only Russian conservatism stood between the Old Order and revolution."[23] At the same time, Kolko argues that the western fear of "international communism" ("an abstraction which existed only in a few Leninist tracts and the minds of frightened statesmen"[24]) amounted to an obsession which had no correspondence in political reality. Thus Kolko manages to have it both ways. Although the Soviets presumably saved the day for the United States in Western Europe by bidding the Communist parties to cooperate in the restoration of the pre-war status quo, American leaders were nevertheless little short of pathological in their belief that the Soviet Union exercised a controlling influence over these parties (for that is what "Communist internationalism" meant). Obviously, this argument will not do. If Bolshevism was our great deliverer in Western Europe, as Kolko contends, the belief in "Communist internationalism" was altogether reasonable at the time. Moreover, even if we accept the view that the Soviets exercised a conservative and restraining influence over the left during the wartime period, how could we be sure they would continue to do so once the necessities imposed by the war had disappeared?

A threat to the stability and security of Western Europe was not equated simply with the possibility of Soviet expansion beyond Eastern Europe. That threat was seen to follow from the division of the

[23] *Ibid.*, p. 450.
[24] *Ibid.*, p. 323.

continent itself. American opposition to this division, with all the momentous consequences to which our opposition led, cannot plausibly be explained (as Williams seeks to do in *The Tragedy of American Diplomacy*) in terms of the trading and investment opportunities in Eastern Europe thereby denied to American business. The evident disproportion of possible benefits to obvious risks renders the explanation not only implausible but absurd. This opposition can be plausibly explained, however, by the belief that the economic recovery, political stability, and, consequently, the peace and security of Western Europe depended upon a continent that was not divided. There is little question that the belief was seriously held by American leaders. Indeed, some radical critics not only emphasize the significance of this belief as a determinant of policy, in their own way they even grant its validity. Thus Kolko finds the root of America's Eastern European policy in the belief that Eastern Europe would remain economically critical for Western Europe. Kolko also shares the belief. "Historically," he writes, "Eastern Europe had been critical to the entire European economy, and this was no less true in 1945."[25] In fact, the critical importance of Eastern Europe to Western Europe was not only less true in 1945; it was never true. Of relevance here, however, is the point that if it were true, as Kolko believes, then America did have a vital security interest in preventing the division of the continent. Whether valid or not, acknowledgment that the belief was seriously held must undermine the assertion that American policy was not, and could not

[25] *Politics of War*, p. 425.

THE RADICAL CRITIQUE ASSESSED

have been, motivated by conventional security considerations.[26]

In part, then, the answer to the radical critique is not that American leaders opposed Soviet policy in Eastern Europe simply because they regarded as illegitimate the security interests that policy sought to achieve (though this they may have done), or even because they regarded as illegitimate the methods by which the Soviets sought to achieve them (though this they surely did), but because they believed that the circumstances in which those interests were sought meant that achieving them would endanger vital American interests.[27] The reasoning went as follows.

[26] Other revisionist critics have emphasized the importance of this belief for American statesmen while giving it a rather broader significance. Gar Alperovitz has pointed to the manner in which President Truman and his secretary of state, Henry Stimson, viewed America's peace and security as dependent on Europe's peace and security, and the latter's peace and security as in turn dependent upon bringing together "the Eastern and Western halves of the European economic unit." *Atomic Diplomacy: Hiroshima and Potsdam* (1965), pp. 78–79. Lloyd C. Gardner notes that "few American leaders seriously believed that East European markets and investments were worth all that fuss .... Americans did believe that the resumption of normal prewar, East-West trade ... was essential to the full recovery of Europe, and thus important generally to American wellbeing and security." *The Origins of the Cold War* (1970), pp. 31–32.

[27] The point is decisive and, in part, explains the distinction that was drawn at the time between America's sphere of influence in the Western Hemisphere and the Soviet Union's sphere of influence in Eastern Europe. It emerges in the clumsy conversation between Henry Stimson and John McCloy, cited by Kolko, pp. 470–73, though that conversation also reveals the ease with which American leaders have assumed that our spheres of influence are somehow qualitatively different from the spheres of influence established by others. It is also worth recalling that in a well-known critique of America's post-war policy, which radical critics are fond of citing, Walter Lippmann

103

An unstable and insecure Western Europe would be one over which the Soviet Union might eventually be able to extend its control. Despite America's present power preponderance, Soviet control over Western Europe might shift the world balance of power against the United States and thus in time create a threat to America's physical security. At the very least, the emergence of Soviet-controlled regimes in Western Europe could be expected to result in a security problem the solution of which would strain the nation's resources and jeopardize its institutions.

In retrospect, a case can be made that this reasoning exaggerated the dependence of American security, particularly America's physical security, on Western Europe. It is neither surprising nor unreasonable, however, that it did not appear so at the time. For America of the middle to late forties, the most relevant experience was the period before and during World War II, an experience seen to demonstrate convincingly the threat to American security that would result from a hostile power in control of Europe, or, still worse, of a hostile power or combination of powers in control of Eurasia. Nor was this experience confined to the threat held out by a victory of the Axis powers. It was also seen in terms of the period 1939–41, when the prospect of a Eurasia partitioned and jointly controlled by Germany, Russia, and Japan could not be lightly dismissed. A revival of that prospect, though now with the Soviet Union as its sole architect and director, was widely consid-

---

endorsed the view that the continued division of Europe held out the danger that "all western Europe might fall within the Russian sphere of influence and be dominated by the Soviet Union." *The Cold War—A Study in U.S. Foreign Policy* (1947), p. 36.

ered to pose a serious threat even to a then preponderant America.

The radical critics are quite right in concluding that the reasons that ultimately impelled us to intervene in World War II also impelled us to a course of action that made the cold war inevitable. On both occasions, the prospect was held out of a world outside this hemisphere hostile to American institutions and interests, a world in which America's economic and political frontiers might become increasingly coextensive with its territorial frontiers, and thus a world in which prosperity and democracy in America itself might be imperiled. The issue of physical security apart, on both occasions it was to prevent this prospect from becoming a reality that either war or the risk of war was undertaken. As in the case of intervention in World War II, the threat that prompted America's cold war policy evidently followed from the manner in which American leaders defined the nation's security in its greater than physical dimension. Was the post-war definition mistaken? Could the projected consequences of a Soviet Union in control of Europe have been avoided if only American policy had not been committed to the expansionist goals of the Open Door? A radical critique does not demonstrate why these questions must be answered affirmatively. It simply asserts that the circumstances in which the questions might have been meaningful never arose.

Security was a principal motive of American policy in the period in which the cold war was joined. Under the circumstances, security apprehensions were not unreasonable, though they were exaggerated. At the same time, American policy was also expansionist, and it was so whether it is viewed in

its objective or in its subjective meaning. That its
objective meaning was expansionist is admitted by
a conventional historiography. What is not generally admitted is that it was expansionist in motive
or intent. Thus the conventional judgment, already
noted, that America's post World War II empire
came into being by accident, that nobody planned
or wanted it. There is a measure of truth in this
judgment. The speed with which America's post-war
expansion occurred, the means by which it was carried out, and the complacency with which it was
viewed, may in part be explained as the unforeseen
and unintended results of the search for security.
Once the cold war was fully joined, this expansion
followed the seemingly inescapable dynamic of hegemonial conflict in which the intensity of the conflict is matched by its ubiquity.

Even so, the theme of the "accidental empire" has
been carried to excess by a conventional historiography. Unless the view is taken that as a nation
America is something new under the sun, our post-
war expansion must ultimately be traced to our inordinate power and to our determination to use this
power to ensure our particular version of a congenial international order. During World War II
abundant evidence of this determination antedates
serious conflict with our major ally. To be sure, once
that conflict arose the security interest could no
longer be separated from the more general interest
in employing our power to sustain a world favorable to American institutions and interests. But such
separation would have proved difficult in any event,
given the generous manner in which the nation's security in its greater than physical sense was defined.
For this definition was practically indistinguishable

from a world stabilized in a pro-American equilibrium.

The radical critic, aware of the expansionist purposes to which our security claims have been put, thereby concludes that what was presented as a security interest was, in reality, little more than a rationalization for expansion. Nearer the truth, it would seem, is that our post-war policy expressed both a conventional security interest and an interest that went well beyond a conventional notion of security. The Truman Doctrine forms the most striking expression of this underlying ambiguity. By interpreting security as a function not only of a balance of power between states but of the internal order maintained by states, and not only by some states but by all states, the Truman Doctrine equated America's security with interests that evidently went well beyond conventional security requirements. This equation cannot be dismissed as mere rhetoric, designed at the time only to mobilize public opinion in support of limited policy actions, though rhetoric taken seriously by succeeding administrations. Instead, it accurately expressed the magnitude of America's conception of its role and interests in the world from the very inception of the cold war. If this is kept in mind, American policy in the fifties and, even more, in the sixties appears not as a perversion of the conception of role and interests that dominated the early period of the cold war, as a conventional historiography maintains, but as its logical progression.

* * *

Thus, the radical account of the origins of the cold war reveals a partial, though nonetheless important, insight that a conventional historiography tends to obscure. Although the radical critic will not see the security interest in post-war American policy, he sees the expansionist interest only too clearly. That the deliberate quality of this interest is exaggerated, that the consistency with which it was presumably translated into early post-war policy is overdrawn, does not invalidate the radical's insistence that America's universalism has been throughout indistinguishable from America's expansionism.

In the period that has followed the initial years of the cold war, it is the expansionist interest that has become increasingly dominant. It was not always so. A conventional security interest was, if not paramount, then of equal significance in the early policy of containment. As initially applied to Europe, containment was more or less synonymous with a balance-of-power policy. Even in an earlier period, though, a narrower and more traditional concept of security coexisted uneasily with a much broader conconcept and one that implied expansion. In part, then, the contrast conventional critics have so often drawn between the relatively precise and limited purposes of early post-war policy and the globalism of American policy in the 1960s is instead a contrast between the circumstances attending the application of policy then and now. For the circumstances of an earlier period limited the application of containment principally to Europe and made that application, whatever its larger purpose, roughly identical with a balance-of-power policy.

This rough identity of containment with a conventional security interest was questionable by the middle 1950s. A decade later, it ceased to have any real plausibility. Vietnam and the ensuing debate illuminated what should long have been apparent, that a profound change had occurred in the structure of American security and that, in consequence, many, if not most, of America's present interests and commitments were largely the result of a concept of security that could no longer satisfactorily account for these same interests and commitments. A continued emphasis on security, remarkable if only because of its excessiveness, could not obscure the fact that security in its more conventional and limited sense had ceased to be of paramount concern. An emphasis on security that often seemed almost inversely proportional to the security interests at stake may be explained by the continued need to justify policy—particularly the employment of force—in terms of interests which no longer defined this policy.

The triumph of an expansionist and imperial interest over an interest that expressed a narrower and more traditional concept of security reflected a change in circumstances rather than, or as much as, a change in essential outlook. It reflected the relative success of the early policy of containment. It also reflected the expansion—concomitant with that success—of American interests and the diversity of possible threats to those interests. By a dialectic as old as the history of statecraft, expansion proved to be the other side of the coin of containment. To contain the expansion of others, or what was perceived as such, it became necessary to expand ourselves. In this manner, the course of containment became the course of empire. In the same manner, the narrower interest containment expressed was submerged in the larger interest of maintaining a stable world order that would ensure the triumph of liberal-capitalist values.

109

Given the nature of this larger interest and the world in which it has been sought, there is no mystery in America's policy of intervention against radical revolution. In an earlier period of the cold war, an interventionist policy could not be separated from the power struggle with the Soviet Union. Even in an earlier period, however, this policy also served a larger interest. The significance of this larger interest because apparent when it was no longer plausible to equate the expansion of communism with the expansion of Soviet (or Chinese) power—yet a policy of intervention not only persisted but, if anything, intensified.[28] It did so because the revolutions that are likely to occur threaten this larger interest.

The revolutions that are likely to occur today hold out the prospect of a greater degree of international instability. More important, they promise to result in the reduction of American influence in the world. The abandonment of an interventionist policy will improve the chances for the emergence to power in the developing nations of regimes that are, if not Communist, at least strongly nationalist and collectivist in character. That these regimes will act independently and in terms of their own interests does not mean that their interests will prove congenial to American interests. However complete their independence of action, their very existence will reduce America's influence and thereby threaten

---

[28] There is room for argument over the point in time when this equation became implausible. Those who are wise after the event will place the point somewhere in the middle to late fifties. It was not unreasonable, however, that men could take the equation seriously until the time of the Cuban missile crisis.

110

the larger interest with which America has come to identify its integrity and well-being.

An interventionist policy is not simply the result, then, of an ideological obsession that is pursued for its own sake. Nor does it stem from intellectual failure. A conventional critique in putting forth these explanations of American policy gives to this policy a quality of disinterestedness it does not possess. It gives to this policy a quality of innocence, however mistaken and even deadly, it does not have. It finds America's opposition to revolutionary movements in the apprehension that these movements will prove to be radical rather than in the apprehension that they will prove resistant to American influence and control. But American policy cannot be adequately explained in terms of an abstract ideological commitment that is divorced from interest and otherwise oblivious to political realities. It may be accounted for in terms of a reasonably well-grounded fear that the American example might become irrelevant to much of the world. The prospect of America's irrelevance as a model for the developing states in turn holds out the prospect of a diminishing influence in and control over these states. America's interventionist and counterrevolutionary policy is the expected response of an imperial power with a vital interest in maintaining an order that, apart from the material benefits this order confers, has become synonymous with the nation's vision of its role in history. Yet this vision cannot be understood in ideological terms alone. In the manner of all imperial visions, it is also solidly rooted in the will to exercise dominion over others. Opposition to radical revolution is to be explained as much by the expectation that such revolution, if successful, will prove resistant to American control as by the fact that the revolution is radical. (This distinction remains significant even if the policy results are largely the same. If nothing else, it places in clearer perspective the role of anticommunism as a determinant of policy. It also suggests that our support of rightist regimes is to be explained much less by the fact that they are rightist than by the conviction—or expectation—that rightist regimes can be controlled.[29])

A radical critique cannot consistently accept this explanation. It cannot consistently accept the view that an interventionist and counterrevolutionary policy has been motivated more by the prospect that the American example, and, in consequence, American influence, might otherwise become irrelevant than by the prospect that in a hostile world America would no longer enjoy the material benefits her hegemonial position has conferred. Yet it is increas-

[29] To illustrate America's persistent opposition to radical revolution and her equally persistent support for rightist regimes, radical critics are fond of citing the statement Arthur Schlesinger, Jr., attributes to President Kennedy shortly after the assassination of Trujillo. Schlesinger reports Kennedy as feeling there were "three possibilities in descending order of preference: a decent democratic regime, a continuation of the Trujillo regime, or a Castro regime." Kennedy concluded: "We ought to aim at the first, but we really can't renounce the second until we are sure that we can avoid the third." *A Thousand Days* (1965), p. 769. But what are we to conclude from this? Surely not that we favored Trujillo-type regimes, all other things being equal, for Kennedy explicitly says the contrary. The statement can only be reasonably interpreted to mean that, in the first place, the power requirements of the struggle with the Soviet Union took precedence over the commitment to a "decent democratic regime." It may be argued that it was mistaken to have calculated in this way, but that is another matter. There is, however, a second sense in which the statement can be understood. The Soviet Union apart, and the power requirements of that struggle apart, there was the issue of permitting a regime

ingly difficult to find in the latter prospect (assuming it to be such) a plausible explanation of why we persist in a counterrevolutionary policy. It is now apparent that the costs of pursuing this policy may be expected to outweigh the material benefits. Indeed, if Vietnam is considered indicative of the future costs of maintaining American hegemony, as radical critics insist, it would seem absurd to continue to account for this policy primarily in terms of the material benefits it may be expected to confer. This is so even if we grant the assumption that these benefits must be calculated primarily in terms of the interests of America's "corporate rulers" rather than the public at large. (Even for a radical critique there is a point beyond which an imperialist policy cannot be rationalized by the argument that the costs of imperialism are borne by the public at large while

---

to come to power that would prove hostile to us, that would refuse to do our bidding, and that—along with Castro—would stand as a challenge to our otherwise undisputed hegemony in this hemisphere. On this basis alone, we would prefer a Trujillo to a Castro, though again not because of any sympathy for the kind of regime Trujillo symbolized. Finally, it is quite true, as Gar Alperovitz has pointd out, there are the constraints imposed by domestic political life which have made it politically hazardous to risk appearing soft on communism. *Cold War Essays* (1970), p. 77. These constraints—these "deeper political forces inherent in American society," to use Alperovitz's words—are clearly important, or, at least, they have been so in the past. But they scarcely bear out the radical view. If anything, they appear more to support a conventional critique. Besides, it needs to be remembered that the gravity of the "soft on communism" charge coincided largely with the active period of the cold war (and even during this period one suspects that it was manipulated as much by politicians who wanted to pursue certain policies as it imprisoned them). Whether it will continue to outlive the cold war, other than in the most attenuated form, remains to be seen. That its potency has substantially declined since the middle of the sixties cannot be doubted.

113

the benefits accrue to those corporations which have international interests. The costs of imperialism may prove harmful to the greater economy, thus creating dissension among the corporate rulers. Even in a Leninist view of imperialism there is no basis for the assumption that any and every imperialist venture will serve the collective interests of the capitalist ruling class. Moreover, once one departs from the dogma that the government of a Capitalist society is nothing but the executive committee of the ruling class, it is apparent that the costs of imperialism to the collective must be taken into consideration.)

There is, of course, the possibility of explaining a policy of counterrevolution largely in terms of false conviction. Confronted with the immensity of our commitment in Vietnam, yet unwilling to attribute this commitment to the varied motives and interests that have customarily defined imperial policies, a growing number of radical critics find our obsession with "stamping out political heresy" rooted in a "messianic ideology . . . that has acquired a force and persuasiveness of its own, quite independent of the political and economic interests underlying it."[30] This view, as we have already shown, is

---

[30] Christopher Lasch, introduction to Gar Alperovitz, *Cold War Essays*, p. 15. Lasch no more believes that American policy is rooted in the independent force of a messianic ideology than does Alperovitz. Instead, both find our counterrevolutionary intervention as essentially rooted in America's system of political economy. Lasch ends his introductory essay by declaring that American policy will change when America adopts a "humane, democratic, and decentralized socialism" (p. 23). Alperovitz insists that we must "restructure fundamentally the deepest American attitudes and institutional patterns at the core of our system of political economy" (p. 121).

indistinguishable in structure from a conventional critique. It differs only in the content given to conviction. Even so, there remains no rational motivation for policy. For this reason alone, a radical critique cannot consistently accept the view that American policy must be understood as rooted primarily in false conviction. Nor does it do so. The same radical critics who stress the independent force of a messianic ideology also insist that fundamental change in foreign policy will come only with a fundamental change in our domestic institutions. It is only with the triumph of a humane socialism that we may hope to cure ourselves of the ideological disease that has so long victimized us. Yet if this is the case, it is not in the independent force of a messianic ideology that we must find the roots of American imperialism but in the institutional structure that has ostensibly given rise to, and continues to sustain, this ideology.

We are left with the one argument which, if well founded, would make plausible what must otherwise appear implausible. It is the argument that the prosperity and, indeed, the very integrity of the American system as it is presently constituted are dependent upon preserving the nation's hegemonial position in the world. This position is not maintained simply because it "pays" but because the American economy cannot do without it. A messianic ideology may support this position. But neither ideology nor imperial pride can explain the apparent persistence in a course of action, as in Vietnam, that has become so costly and so self-defeating. It is only the dependence of a socio-economic order at home on the maintenance of America's present role and interests in the world that can satisfactorily explain the determination of successive administrations not to accept a precedent-setting defeat. Nothing less than the security of an economic and social system requires a policy of counterrevolutionary intervention.

Here as elsewhere, there are variations on the central theme. Thus in the context of Vietnam, our intervention has been explained in terms of the need to keep Vietnam, and Southeast Asia, as a market for Japan. Without Southeast Asia, the argument runs, Japan would be forced to turn increasingly to China as a market for imports and a source of needed raw materials. The eventual result would be the ascendency of Chinese influence over Japan and the beginning of the end of American hegemony in Asia. Carl Oglesby was one of the first to articulate this explanation of why we are in Vietnam.[31] More recently, Noam Chomsky has taken it up.[32] Invariably, the radical argument is attended by citation of the views of American leaders, from President Eisenhower on, who have equated the future of Japan with the future of Southeast Asia and, in turn, with Vietnam. At best, however, citation of these views proves no more than conviction, and a mistaken conviction at that. As a source of raw materials, or as a market for Japanese exports, Southeast Asia can scarcely be considered vital to the postwar Japanese economy.[33] The radical argument

[31] *Vietnamese Crucible*, pp. 113–30.

[32] *New York Review of Books*, Jan. 1, 1970, p. 12; June 4, 1970, p. 50.

[33] In 1969, Japanese imports from Southeast Asia were roughly 9 percent of all Japanese imports and 22 percent of all imports from developing countries. For the same year, Japanese exports to Asian countries were 26 percent, and to Southeast Asian countries 15 percent, of all Japanese exports. Of the percentage of Asian exports, at least half went to South Korea, Taiwan, and Hong Kong. See International Monetary Fund,

of Japanese dependence on Southeast Asia is difficult to take seriously. No less farfetched, it would appear, is the view that China could become in the foreseeable future the principal market for Japanese exports. To the extent the "loss" of Southeast Asia could plausibly be expected to turn Japan toward China, the reason clearly would not be economic but political—that is, the need to accommodate oneself to the hegemonic power of the region. But it is very doubtful that Vietnam (at least after 1964) can be explained as a mistaken conviction of the nature radical critics imply. If there was a mistaken conviction that can in large measure explain Vietnam, it was the conviction that defeat in Vietnam, by paving the way for Chinese expansion over the whole of Southeast Asia, would upset the Asian balance of power and thereby threaten Japan. In turn, it was feared that this threat might result either in turning Japan toward China (though not for economic reasons) or in prompting Japan to embark on an independent, and very possibly militant, policy of her own. If one assumes that this conviction was not mistaken, then there is indeed a great deal to be said for the intervention in Vietnam (however abortive it now may appear).

What is the evidence for the argument of dependence? Clearly, it cannot consist simply in the reassertion of what is essentially a Marxist-Leninist

---

Directions of Trade (1969), pp. 51–53. It should be noted that there are few raw materials the Japanese import from Southeast Asia which could not be imported from other areas and without exorbitant increases in cost. Thus, there are alternatives to Japan's present import patterns relative to Southeast Asia, although why Southeast Asia—even under Chinese control— would deny Japan needed sources of raw materials is not easy to see.

view respecting the nature and requirements of a Capitalist economy. Whether the American economy is, for example, critically dependent upon its position of privileged consumer of the world's raw materials cannot be established by yet another radical inquiry into the nature of capitalism. Instead, it must be shown that without continued access to foreign sources of raw materials the American economy either could not function as presently constituted or could not do so at anywhere close to the present level (including, of course, present rates of growth). Even then, the kind of dependence that could plausibly account for an interventionist policy would have to show that access to foreign sources of raw materials would likely be jeopardized were America to abandon an interventionist policy. (At least, this would have to be shown if we are to assume some semblance of rationality on the part of those who determine policy.) It is only rare, however, that radical critics even seriously attempt to make this kind of case for dependency, whether with respect to raw materials or with respect to investment and trade. Instead, their case is characteristically an indiscriminate mixture of assertions which presumably establish America's dependency on the maintenance of the empire and unprovable hypotheses about the inherent nature of capitalism.

In this respect, Harry Magdoff's *The Age of Imperialism* may be taken as representative. Magdoff's argument is designed to establish that our foreign economic involvement is critical to the functioning of the American economy as it is presently constituted. Is American policy, *for this reason*, of necessity imperialist? Magdoff will not say so. Instead, he takes the argument of dependence, in this narrower sense of the term, as far as it will carry him (and, as we shall presently see, a good deal farther than it can legitimately carry him), whereupon he then argues the case for dependence—hence for imperialism—in terms of the inherent nature of a Capitalist system. The argument of dependence must therefore be understood in a narrower and a broader sense, or, in what we would term, an economic and a meta-economic sense. Raw materials provide an example of this method of analysis. In part, the need for external sources of raw materials and the determination to insure access to these sources is attributed either to their scarcity or to their low price. On this view, we are dependent on certain raw materials in the narrower sense of the term—that is, we must have them either to produce what we are presently producing (let alone to ensure future growth) or to produce what we are producing at a reasonable price. In part, however, the need presumably arises because of the nature of capitalism, above all in its monopolistic stage. When pressed to defend the case for dependence in the narrower sense, Magdoff falls back on the case for dependence in the broader sense. Elsewhere he has written: "The issue . . . is not dependency of the United States on foreign mineral supplies, but the dependency of monopoly industry *qua* 'monopolies' on the control of these supplies."[34] Thus one has the best of both worlds. If dependence in the narrower sense fails, it is always possible to fall back on the broader meaning. In the latter meaning our dependence arises from the nature of monopoly capitalism which *must* control as much of the world's resources of raw materials as

[34] *Monthly Review* (Nov., 1970), p. 6.

possible. And since the government is but the willing servant of monopoly capitalism, the dependency of the United States on raw materials is, in the last analysis, the dependency of "monopoly industry *qua* monopolies."

The reasons for the unwillingness to deal with the argument of dependency in anything less than the broadest of frameworks become apparent once the radical case is examined. For if the nature of capitalism is set aside, not only does the evidence fail to bear out the argument of dependency but it points in the opposite direction to an economy that is remarkably self-sufficient, so much so that a policy of autarky represents a very real possibility (however undesirable the economic and, even more, the political consequences of such a policy). No doubt, a policy of autarky, or something closely akin to autarky, would require a period of time during which the changes autarky implies could be absorbed. There are no persuasive reasons for assuming, however, that these changes could not be absorbed. Nor are there persuasive—or even plausible—reasons for assuming that they might have to be undertaken without the benefit of time. The radical argument gains a limited measure of persuasiveness only if it is assumed that there would be no time for adjustment. But in the absence of a global conflict, the scenario of a sudden and complete denial of access to foreign sources of raw materials is as much a fantasy as is the projection of a sudden and complete loss of foreign investment (or the severance of foreign trade). In the event of a global conflict, which would by definition involve the great nuclear powers, the prospective sacrifice of America's foreign economic interests is likely to be among the least of the catastrophes besetting the nation.

These conclusions, which are as unpalatable to many radical critics as they are to orthodox champions of interdependence,[35] may be illustrated by considering the nature and extent of America's dependence on raw materials. (Those who object to defining the problem in these terms are free to substitute capitalism or monopoly capitalism for America.) To what extent is America's dependence on foreign sources of raw materials just that, a dependence, or no more than a significant convenience? The radical critic assumes that our present pattern of imports[36] clearly establishes the case for depend-

---

[35] Cf. Kenneth N. Waltz, "The Myth of National Interdependence" in *The International Corporation*, ed. by Charles Kindelberger (1970), pp. 205–23. Waltz writes that "the American rhetoric of interdependence has taken on some of the qualities of an ideology. The word 'interdependence' subtly obscures the inequalities of national capability, pleasingly points to a reciprocal dependence, and strongly suggests that all states are playing the same game" (p. 220). This is the orthodox ideology of interdependence, the rhetoric of which is common to government spokesmen and business leaders. The radical rhetoric, though insistent upon the inequalities of national capability and emphatic that states are playing a very different game, nevertheless shares much the same fundamental assumption of reciprocal dependence.

[36] In terms of the *value* of minerals and mineral products imported and exported by the United States in 1968, imports in crude metals represented 65% of the total and in manufactured metals 76% of the total. *Minerals Yearbook, 1968*, Department of the Interior, p. 34. The standard work on America's raw materials needs, though already somewhat dated, is Hans L. Landsberg, Leonard L. Fischman, and Joseph L. Fisher, *Resources in America's Future: Patterns of Requirements and Availabilities, 1960–2000* (1963). The political detachment of

ence. Moreover, this dependence cannot be measured simply in terms of volume or even of price. It must also be seen in qualitative or absolute terms, that is, in terms of scarce raw materials the needed quantities of which may be small but without which an industry cannot function. The economy of the United States is so intricate, Gabriel Kolko writes, "that the removal of even a small part, as in a watch, can stop the mechanism. The steel industry must add approximately thirteen pounds of manganese to each ton of steel, and though the weight and value of the increase is a tiny fraction of the total, a modern diversified steel industry *must* have manganese."[37] To Kolko's example of manganese may be added Harry Magdoff's example of the six critical materials needed to make a jet engine, and all of which, with the exception of one, we are dependent on imports for an adequate supply.[38]

Bad examples may not discredit a general argument, but they do tell us something about the argument. That manganese is necessary for steel production, that we presently rely largely on foreign sources, that approximately one-half the world's present reserves are located in Communist countries, and that the projected demand of manganese is placed at 300 million tons while present reserves are calculated at 185 million tons—these are all facts. Do any of these facts support the general conclu-

---

the study by Landsberg, *et al*, contrasts markedly with earlier studies which are intent on establishing America's critical dependence on foreign sources of raw materials and which, in consequence, were used as a justification for cold war policy. Understandably, radical critics are fond of citing these studies.

[37] *The Roots of American Foreign Policy*, p. 50.
[38] *The Age of Imperialism*, pp. 50–53.

sions the radical argument draws? It would not seem so. At present, manganese is being increasingly recovered from the waste materials discarded from the steel-making process. Recently, vast resources of manganese have been found on the ocean's floor. Even if it is assumed that the exploitation of manganese on the ocean's floor will prove costly, and the evidence for this is lacking, the added cost can have no more than a marginal effect on the price of steel. These considerations apart, there are no plausible reasons for believing that in the foreseeable future we will have trouble obtaining manganese from such diverse sources as Brazil, India, South Africa, and Japan. For that matter, Communist states have shown no reluctance to sell manganese to the United States. A sense of security is evidenced by present consumption statistics which show a decline in consumption, imports, and world price of manganese.

The example of the jet engine materials fares no better than manganese. These ferroalloys, which are used to strengthen steel, are: tungsten, colombium, nickel, chromium, molybdenum, and cobalt. Of these materials, molybdenum is the only one the United States possesses in abundance. Does it matter a great deal? Apparently not, since in the face of projected shortages, any ferroalloy can be made adequately substitutable for another. Thus if chromium should ever be denied us, molybdenum and vanadium, both of which are plentiful in the United States, could be substituted. But why should chromium be denied us when among the major producers in the non-Communist world are South Africa, Turkey, Rhodesia, and the Philippines? Once again, a sense of security —of independence—is evidenced by a depressed market for ferroalloys and by the seeming uncon-

cern with which the United States is letting its once
formidable stockpile of "strategic materials" de-
teriorate.

A generally optimistic raw materials picture for
the near future may be, and frequently is, chal-
lenged by projected estimates of consumption run-
ning to the year 2000 and even beyond. For our
purposes, it is unnecessary to raise the question of
how seriously these projections should be taken,
based as they are on present technology and present
consumption patterns. Of relevance in this context is
the much more limited issue of the significance of
import patterns in determining America's dependence on foreign sources of raw materials, and particularly those sources located in the Third World.
If the above examples are taken as at all representative of the raw materials problem, they point to
the conclusion that in America's case a high rate of
imports by no means establishes the case for dependency. Given our present import pattern, one may of
course still speak of America as "heavily dependent"
upon the import of raw materials. But there is a
world of difference between a dependence which indicates only that imports form a high percentage of
consumption and a dependence which indicates the
absence of any alternatives to this import pattern.
The former proves no more than a relative dependence, that is, a convenience, whereas the latter alone
proves an absolute dependence.

That there are alternatives to the present import
pattern of raw materials can scarcely be disputed.
What can be disputed is the degree of inconvenience
they would impose, largely in terms of higher prices,
and the extent to which they would reduce present
rates of import. In the case of most raw materials,

it is clear that the problem is one of convenience, since the United States possesses them in abundant quantities. For these materials, scarcity means scarcity of high yield deposits. If and when high-yield deposits abroad should be shut off, lower yield deposits at home would presumably be exploited. How inconvenient this might prove to be in terms of cost would depend upon a number of factors. An advancing metals technology may almost certainly be expected to reduce significantly the inconvenience. Technology has come to affect every aspect of production, from detecting new reserves and processing poorer grades of ore competitively to finding methods of reducing the metals content in finished products while maintaining quality. Technology may also be expected to further improve the methods by which materials are recovered and recycled. Finally, technological advances leave almost open-ended the prospects for substitution, whether vertical (one mineral for another) or horizontal (a synthetic substance for a mineral). These technological advances may eventually be expected to benefit the developing states as well. Those who insist upon the grave harm done to these states by depriving them of their natural resources often neglect this point.

Given a sufficient period of time, then, there is the alternative of relying on our own resources and even of doing so at relatively little inconvenience. Let us assume, however, that this alternative would prove very costly and, even more, that for a number of needed raw materials it could not be undertaken at all. Would this assumption plausibly account for a counterrevolutionary America? The radical argument concludes that it would and does. The conclusion is unfounded if only because it neglects the sig-

nificance of the sources of our raw materials, which
are not only numerous but which, in the main, are
also situated in safe areas. The number of suppliers
alone is probably sufficient as insurance against pro-
hibitive prices. There remains the possibility of out-
right denial. But even if we set aside the secure
sources of raw materials, why should revolutionary,
and otherwise hostile, regimes deny us (or the other
industrial nations) their raw materials? Surely they
would not do so out of devotion to revolutionary
ideals. Radical intellectuals may harbor such romantic notions but governments, revolutionary governments included, do not. Only slightly less romantic
is the idea that revolutionary regimes would take a
very different view of their heritage of natural resources. Apart from exercising direct control over
their natural resources and attempting to obtain a
better price for them on the international market, it
is difficult to know what this different view might be.
Revolutionary regimes will still need foreign capital.
So long as raw material exports provide a principal
means for obtaining foreign capital, there is little
reason for believing that the resources of revolutionary regimes will be denied to America.

In the case of investments, the sheer magnitude
of America's foreign economic involvement gives the
radical argument of dependency an apparent plausibility. In 1969, American investments abroad, official
and private, were valued at $158 billion, with pri-
vate investments ($110 billion) making up approxi-
mately two-thirds of the total. Direct investment in
branches and subsidiaries of U.S. enterprises abroad,
the critical category of private foreign investment,
was valued at $70.8 billion. Moreover, the figures

on private investment represent book value, which is substantially below true market value.[39]

American investment abroad is not only impressive in its sheer magnitude, it also reveals a dramatic rate of growth. From 1960 to 1969 direct investment increased 122%. In 1968, total new assets, which includes net reinvested earnings of businesses abroad, was $11.4 billion, an increase of 60.4% over 1966. In 1969, new private direct investment was $7.6 billion, an increase of 48% over 1966. Whether the growth of recent years may be expected to continue in the future is a matter of some debate and uncertainty. There is no question, though, of the very considerable impact of American direct investments both in the world economy and in the economies of individual countries. One indication of this impact may be seen in the gross value of the output of American firms operating abroad. Calculated at over $120 billion in 1967, this output ranked ahead of all but the two largest national economies.[40]

However large American investment abroad ap-

[39] Unless otherwise noted, the figures in this section are taken from the Commerce Department's *Survey of Current Business*, October 1969, pp. 23–36, and October, 1970, pp. 21–37, as well as relevant sections of the *Statistical Abstract of the United States*, 1969. There is no agreed-upon formula for translating the book value of investments into their true market value. Since, however, we are primarily concerned here with the significance of foreign investment relative to the domestic economy, the question of the real worth of foreign investment is not one of great moment. Estimates of domestic investment also represent book values. In concentrating largely on direct investment, we do so because it is direct investment that forms the major category of private foreign investment and that actively influences the economy, and politics, of other countries.

[40] Waltz, *The Myth of Interdependence*, pp. 217–18. Japan has since exceeded this output, if indeed it had not done so in 1967.

pears when measured in absolute terms, and however great the impact of this investment on others, its significance for the domestic economy must of course be understood primarily in terms relative to this economy. In 1968, gross private domestic investment was $127.7 billion, on a base of $1.6 trillion in total corporate assets. Direct investment abroad as a percentage of total investment was roughly 6%. Viewed in still another way, the value of private investment abroad (direct and portfolio) in 1968 represented 8% of total corporate assets for that year. Again, in 1968, the return on total private investment abroad was $8.6 billion. When compared with domestic corporate profits of $92.3 billion, the return on foreign investment was 9.3% of domestic corporate profits.[41] Viewed simply in absolute terms, the magnitude of American private in-

----

[41] In the above calculation of return on foreign private investment, we have chosen to follow Magdoff, *The Age of Imperialism*, p. 183. Our "return" equals Magdoff's "earnings" in that both include income on direct investment, re-invested earnings, other earnings (in the main, portfolio), royalties, and fees. Even so, if we had followed Magdoff's method of calculating the return on foreign investment as a percentage of domestic corporate profits the result would have been very different. Magdoff minimizes domestic corporate profits by quoting profits after taxes. (For example, in the year Magdoff takes, 1964, corporate profits before taxes were $53.7 billion and after taxes $31.3 billion.) In addition, Magdoff's profits include only nonfinancial domestic corporations. But his earnings on foreign investment are quoted before U.S. taxes and include earnings on investments made by financial corporations. By comparing these incomparables, Magdoff can arrive at the conclusion that in 1964 "foreign sources of earnings accounted for about 22 percent of domestic nonfinancial corporate profits." If Magdoff has quoted domestic corporate profits before taxes and included domestic financial corporations, foreign earnings as a percentage of domestic earnings would be roughly one-third the figure he cites.

vestment abroad may prove very misleading as an indication of its significance for the domestic economy.

It may of course be argued that these percentages, while seemingly modest, are nevertheless crucial, in that without the outlet provided by foreign investment (though only 6%) and the earnings obtained from abroad (9.3% of total corporate profits) the American economy could not function at anywhere near its present levels. If the argument is impossible to substantiate, it may be conceded that it is also difficult to disprove. Is it necessary, however, to make the effort to disprove it? It would not seem so, if for no other reason than the geographical location of American investments.

It is not in the Third World, the low-income states, that the bulk of American assets and investments are to be found, but in Western Europe (30%), Canada (29%), Australia, New Zealand, and South Africa (6%), and Japan (2%). These states are the home of $47.7 billion in direct investment, with only $20 billion invested in all of the low income states (with $13 billion of the $20 billion in Latin America). In 1969, the developed- and Capitalist-countries accounted for $4.2 billion of the $5.8 billion growth in the book value of direct investment. In contrast, direct investment rose only $1.2 billion in the lesser developed areas. These figures continue a trend observable throughout the 1960s of a steady decline in the percentage of direct investment in poor states. Whereas in 1960 the latter had 40% of American direct investment, in 1969 the percentage had shrunk to 30%.

It is true that returns on investments from the underdeveloped states are proportionately higher than returns from investments located in developed states. For the most part, this disparity is to be explained by the high concentration of investment in petroleum. In 1969, 41% of American private investment in low-income countries was in petroleum. At the same time, the earnings from investment in petroleum ($2.4 billion) represented 61% of the earnings from all investment in these countries ($4 billion). The special case of oil excluded, in 1969 the rates of return on manufacturing investments between industrial and non-industrial areas were about the same. Even if the high returns on oil are included, the earnings on investments from the non-industrial areas have in recent years formed a slightly decreasing percentage of earnings on private foreign investment as a whole.

The October, 1970, issue of *Survey of Current Business* states: "With the rise in the rate of return on manufacturing investments abroad to 12.8% in 1969, the rate of return of 12.6% on comparable domestic investments was exceeded for the first time in a number of years. Over the past ten years yields on domestic investment averaged 12.4%, only slightly higher than the 11.8% average on direct investments abroad."[42] These percentages included all manufacturing investments abroad. The *Survey* goes on to note that rates of return on manufacturing investments between industrial and nonindustrial areas "are about the same." Inasmuch, then, as the charge of exploitation held to attend investment in undeveloped areas rests on the presumed marked disparity in rates of return on domestic and foreign investment, it must concentrate largely on oil (and to a much lesser degree on mining and smelting). The

[42] *Survey of Current Business* (Oct., 1970), p. 32.

case of oil is of course a very special one not only because it accounts for so much of the earnings from undeveloped areas and enjoys a rate of return that is inordinately higher than manufactures (and minerals), but also because of the industry's evident dependence on overseas profits. Concentrated in the Middle East, the book value alone of the American investment in this area is between $2 and $3 billion and its net benefit to the United States balance of payments is $1.5 billion. Given the radical view, one would expect that here, if anywhere, American policy would faithfully reflect economic interests. The reality, as is well known, is otherwise. Apart from the increasing and successful pressures oil countries have employed to increase their royalty and tax income (pressures which have not provoked any notable countermeasures), the American government has contributed to the steady deterioration of the favorable position American oil companies once enjoyed in the Middle East. A *New York Times* correspondent, John M. Lee, writes: "The remarkable thing to many observers is that the oil companies and oil considerations have had such little influence in American foreign policy toward Israel."[43]

The case of oil apart, if the "crucial" percentages, cited earlier, are to be adjusted to take into account the vulnerability of investments in terms of their geographical location, these percentages must be reduced to a point at which, even for debating purposes, they are clearly no longer crucial. Nor can life be breathed into the radical case respecting investments by pointing to the dependence of investments in developed countries on continued access to

[43] *New York Times*, Jan. 3, 1971, p. 3.

the raw materials of the underdeveloped countries. For this argument not only must raise many of the questions we have already considered when dealing with the alleged dependence of the domestic economy on raw materials, it must raise them in a still more extreme form. Whereas before we had to assume that America would somehow be denied access to needed raw materials, now we have to assume that the entire developed world would similarly be denied access. A condition of global conflict and chaos apart, there is no apparent reason why this assumption should merit serious consideration.

The Marxist critic may well respond to the implications of this discussion by noting that it neglects the imperialist rivalries of advanced Capitalist states, rivalries not only for control of the markets of undeveloped countries but rivalries among the Capitalist states themselves. It is the imperialist rivalries attending the capital flow of the advanced states across one another's borders that is, on this view, the hub of the imperialist wheel. This being the case, the primary issue is not so much whether we can do without investment outlets in the Third World (or whether American capitalism can survive the loss of investments in the Third World), but whether we can do without investment outlets in the advanced states. To this response, the following points may be made. It is first of all clear that there is a fundamental difference between American investment in Europe or Canada and in the Third World. In the former countries, investment does not result in relations of control. Rhetorical exaggeration apart, mature industrial countries cannot be controlled by foreign capital, at least, not in the sense that bears a meaningful comparison to the control that may be exercised over undeveloped countries. Indeed, almost all the charges made with respect to investment in undeveloped countries—that development is impeded or skewed, that scarce capital is pumped out, that labor is exploited (even relative to labor in the metropolis), etc.—are irrelevant in the case of investment in developed countries. More important still for this discussion, however, is that even if we were to term our relations with the advanced states imperialist, by virtue of the hegemonial role of American capital in the North Atlantic economy, this would still fail to explain a policy of counterrevolutionary intervention in the Third World that is not duplicated in the First. Moreover, our policy in the Third World is one our principal Capitalist allies have not chosen to emulate. Why not? The radical response is that there is no need for our principal allies to emulate us, for they are the beneficiaries of our actions. What appears, then, as capitalism without empire (for example, Japan, Germany, etc.), is capitalism with empire by proxy. But this response is difficult to reconcile with the view that our principal Capitalist allies are also our principal adversaries (and today more than ever) in the imperialist network.

Can the need for exports explain what the need for imports (raw materials) and foreign investments fail to explain? Is it plausible to find in the search for foreign markets the roots of an interventionist and counterrevolutionary policy? In radical historiography, we recall, it is this need, real or imagined, that provides the principal explanation of American expansion from the late nineteenth century on. To be sure, the Open Door has also been interpreted to mean access to raw materials and receptivity to foreign investment. Even so, in its earlier stages it is

133

the need to export surplus goods that presumably forms the principal reason for ensuring that wherever possible the door be kept open to American business. The ideology in which, according to radical historians, freedom and world peace came to be equated with an unrestricted international market reflects the key importance given the need to export. It is the same ideology of free trade that forms the central thread of all radical accounts of American diplomacy during and following World War II. Throughout, the driving force of American policy was the conviction that the nation could avoid sliding back into the depression of the pre-war years only if assured of foreign markets capable of absorbing our "unlimited creative energy." And if for a still more recent period the need to export no longer receives quite the same emphasis, it still represents one of the cornerstones of the radical argument.

The same considerations that apply to imports and foreign investments are by and large applicable to exports. Thus it is not enough simply to point out that the export of goods was valued at $34.7 billion for 1968 and that this figure more than tripled in the period from 1950 to 1968. What is relevant here is the significance of exports when taken in relation to the domestic economy. One indication of their significance is that in 1968 they represented roughly 4% of a GNP of $860 billion. Radical critics have argued that this percentage is misleading when used to indicate the significance of exports to the domestic economy, since it compares the value of goods as exports with the domestic value of both goods and services. Whereas the value of exports in relation to GNP is 4%, in relation to the value of goods sold domestically it is 8%. Even if the latter percentage is taken as a more meaningful indication of the significance of exports to the domestic economy, it scarcely bears out the argument of a dependence on exports. Moreover, unless it can be demonstrated that the economy as a whole remains critically dependent upon the goods producing sector, there is no persuasive reason for accepting the latter percentage as the more meaningful one.[44]

Let us assume, however, that the export of goods is critical to the domestic economy as it presently functions and, further, that they were to be cut off. Although neither assumption is plausible, the consequences would still not be those suggested by the radical argument, and for the most apparent of reasons. Against $34.7 billion in exports, 80% of which are made up of five product groups—transportation (mainly aircraft), chemicals, electrical machinery (computers and highly sophisticated office machinery), nonelectrical machinery, and scientific instruments—the United States imported $33.3 billion in 1968, 70% of which comprised manufactures. Assuming that foreign markets were cut off, we may also assume that the domestic market would be— or, at least, could be—closed to foreign manufactures (we leave aside the problem of raw-material imports). The hardship imposed on particular industries apart, the resultant blow to the economy as

[44] The above percentages are calculated from the *Statistical Abstract of the United States*, 1969, p. 310. The relative consistency of goods exported in relation to domestic production may be noted. Exports as a percentage of domestic production are 8.5 for 1930, 6.3 for 1950, 7.1 for 1955, and 8 for 1960. The 8% for 1968 therefore appears to represent something of a norm for recent decades. Nor does it follow that in an increasingly oriented services economy this percentage will show a substantial rise. More likely is the prospect, discussed in the text, that the export of goods will decline.

a whole would be something considerably short of mortal.[45] At a more serious level of analysis, a comparison of exports as a percentage of total output of goods indicates the relatively small amounts involved. Using government input-output tables for 1958 and 1963, we find that only two industries (iron and ferroalloy-ore mining, and scientific instruments) show significant increases for the five-year period, while several industries show a decline. Further, in only two industries (oil field machinery and equipment and construction and mining machinery and equipment) are exports over 20% of the total produced. For most industries, exports not only account for less than 10% of the total output but show decreasing percentages. For the principal product groups cited above, the importance of exports in recent years has declined overall.

Given the structure of American exports, it follows that our trade is predominantly with rich competitors and not with the developing states of the Third World. In 1968, 67% of American exports went to Western Europe, Canada, and Japan. These countries continue to take an ever-increasing percentage of American exports while sharing an ever-increasing percentage of American imports. By contrast, the percentage of American exports to the developing states declined from 37% to 31.3% between 1955 and 1968. With respect to the Third World, then, the parallel between exports and investments (or, for that matter, imports) is clear. It is in the developed nations that America's economic involvement abroad is increasingly concentrated.

[45] We are driven to conjure up this improbable situation because of the radical penchant for emphasizing exports while neglecting imports.

If the significance of goods exported is already marginal by comparison with domestic economic activity, and even quite modest by comparison with goods directly produced abroad by American enterprises, the prospect is for still further decrease in the importance of trade.[46] In an increasingly service-oriented economy, the competitive advantage formerly enjoyed by goods producing industries may be expected to decline. This decline will in all likelihood be subject to certain exceptions, above all, in those industries where technological change places a high premium on the ability to make large expenditures for research and development. Moreover, a continued interest in the export of goods may be expected to persist if only because of the political pressures exerted on behalf of the agricultural sector, which has become increasingly dependent on foreign markets. Although the emergent trade picture must therefore be qualified, the steady movement toward a service economy nevertheless points to an overall decline in the importance of exports. At the same time, the prospect of an adverse trade balance, consequent upon a relative decline of exports and an increase of imports, is one that can be viewed with equanimity, for the returns on American investments abroad will more than compensate for the loss in trade. Thus, even if we were to accept the radical contention that a trade surplus has been necessary in the past to pay for the empire and to maintain American hegemony, there is no reason to assume that the eventual disappearance of this surplus will result in an unfavorable balance of payments for this country. Indeed, it has been suggested that on

[46] Cf. Lawrence Krause, "Trade Policy in the Atlantic World," Brookings Institution, October, 1970.

137

a quite conservative estimate of the returns on American investments, based on current trends of investment and profit, the real question is "how other countries will be able to balance their accounts if the U.S. does not run a substantial trade deficit."[47]

If these considerations fail to shake the radical's argument, it is because that argument is ultimately impervious to them. Indeed, the radical may even concede most of them, yet insist that the need to preserve the option of foreign investment and trade, and to insure access to sources of raw materials, explains America's interventionist and counterrevolutionary policy. This need cannot be understood in the sense we have considered it. Nor can it be satisfied by the kinds of assurances the above discussion has brought forth. At the root of the radical's position is the insistence that the interests which determine American foreign policy cannot be appeased by the prospect of a future that leaves open the door to uncertainty, however small. What these interests require, and demand, is nothing less than complete assurance of maximum freedom of development, an assurance which can be met only by retaining access to, or control over, as much of the world as our power permits. Moreover, that assurance must be met even though the costs appear to exceed the benefits. In the end, the radical argument rests, as always, upon the manner in which a Capitalist America must, by definition, behave.

* * *

Would a Socialist America pursue a foreign policy fundamentally different from the foreign policy pursued by a Capitalist America? Would it no longer

[47] Krause, "Trade Policy in the Atlantic World," pp. 8–10.

seek to influence the course of development of other peoples? Would it abandon its hegemonial position along with the advantages this position has conferred? Would it provide a generous measure of assistance to developing nations while neither seeking nor expecting any tangible advantages in return?

Whether explicitly or implicitly, a radical critique answers these questions affirmatively. Whatever the differences otherwise separating them, the belief that a Socialist America would pursue a fundamentally different foreign policy is common to all radical critics. The pervasiveness of this belief is in itself significant. That it is held with equal fervor by those who nevertheless stress the independent force of conviction in the determination of policy must remain inexplicable, unless conviction is seen as not only having grown out of but as continuing to reflect the socio-economic structure of society.

What may we say of the radical belief? Clearly, a Socialist America would in some respects behave differently from a Capitalist America. It would no longer seek to insure the triumph of liberal-capitalist values. But a radical critique cannot be content with telling us what no one would care to dispute. What many would dispute is the contention that such an America would no longer attempt to control its environment, that it would no longer attempt to fashion some sort of greater order, and that it would no longer entertain imperial relationships with other and weaker states. That these relationships would be undertaken for ostensibly different reasons cannot preclude the prospect that they would still be characterized by inequality and by some form of coercion.

It is not enough, then, to content oneself with saying that a Socialist America would no longer pursue

Capitalist ways. For unless the "ways" of capitalism are equated with the ways collectives have displayed from time immemorial, we might be expected to retain interests that have little to do with capitalism but a great deal to do with the pretensions great powers have almost invariably manifested. If history is to prove at all relevant in this regard, there is no apparent reason to assume that the new America would refrain from identifying the collective self with something larger than the self. If this is so, the nation's security and well-being would still be identified with a world that remained receptive to American institutions and interests. No doubt, a Socialist America would define those institutions and interests in a manner different from the definition of a Capitalist America. But this difference cannot be taken to mean that we would refrain from attempting to influence the course of development of other peoples. The possibility—or, rather, the probability —must be entertained that there would still be revolutions, even radical revolutions, the nature and international consequences of which we might oppose. Nor is there any assurance that our opposition would appear less oppressive to others simply because it was no longer motivated by the desire to safeguard private investments or needed sources of raw materials.

That American policy would no longer be concerned with maintaining an environment receptive to the investment of capital follows by definition. Would the same lack of concern be manifested toward safeguarding present sources of raw materials, particularly if they are as critical to the economy as the radicals contend? Radical critics make a great deal of the political and psychological necessity of a Capitalist America to preserve access to needed sources of raw materials. Why is it assumed that this is a "necessity" unique to capitalism? Is it unreasonable to assume that a Socialist America might also wish to preserve similar access? It may of course be argued that a Socialist America would not consume the quantities of raw materials a Capitalist America consumes and that for those raw materials it still needed to import it would pay a "just" price. But this argument is one that proceeds by definition, that is, by defining how a truly Socialist society would act, rather than by experience.

Let us assume, however, that a Socialist America would not identify its security and well-being with a world that remained receptive to American institutions and interests. Let us assume that the new society would have no incentive to find its fulfillment in foreign policy. Given a physical security that is no longer dependent upon what transpires outside the North American continent, the triumph of socialism would signal, on this assumption, the disappearance of any remaining need to find our security and well-being in the greater than physical sense dependent upon events occurring beyond our frontiers. In these circumstances, it may then be argued, America's economic and political frontiers could at last become coextensive with its territorial frontiers and the compulsion, whether institutional or psychological, to expand and to control our environment would atrophy and, indeed, disappear.

In these same circumstances, however, what would prevent us from disinteresting ourselves in the rest of the world, and particularly in the developing states? Why should it matter to us whether the impoverished remain impoverished, if their fate carries no consequences for our own well-being?[48] On the other hand, if it is argued that our fate is inextricably tied to the fate of the developing states, then even a Socialist America would continue to have a compelling incentive to influence its environment. Then even a Socialist America would not refrain, because it could not safely refrain, from identifying the collective self with something larger than the self. That identification has been a principal source of what justice men have been capable of showing in their collective relations. In a world of unequals, it has also been the source of an interest that has readily assumed imperial dimensions.

The world of a Socialist America would still be a world marked by great inequalities. It would still be a world of the strong and the weak, the rich and the poor. If injustice springs from such inequalities, what are the grounds for believing the new society would act justly toward the weak? It is, after all, not only Capitalist states that have sought to take advantage of their strength when dealing with poor and weak states. The record of the Soviet Union's relations with the underdeveloped states scarcely bears out a reluctance to draw such advantages as it can from its position of strength. It may of course

[48] The response may of course be made that even if we assume a Socialist America would be indifferent to the fate of the impoverished this would still be infinitely preferable to the repressive "concern" of an imperialist America, that between a real neglect and a repressive concern the former must appear quite benign. This response, which is not only made by radicals, cannot be easily dismissed, however much it may exaggerate America's responsibility for the plight of impoverished peoples. Even so, it leaves open the question raised above. At least, it leaves open this question unless we assume that in a truly Socialist society men's sense of sympathy would, at long last, know no boundaries.

142

be argued that this only proves that the Soviet Union is not a truly Socialist state. It may also be argued that the Soviet Union's behavior indicates that the real source of injustice and exploitation today stem from the fact that the world is divided into rich and poor states. The latter argument is a striking departure from Marxism or its Leninist adaptation, but it is still not enough of a departure. It is not only the division of humanity into the rich and the poor that gives rise to the various forms of unequal relationships the radical equates with imperialism. It is also the division of humanity into discrete collectives. If advanced states, whether Capitalist or Socialist, may behave similarly in many respects toward backward states, it is not simply because they are advanced but because collectives have very little sense of obligation to others. That is why we have no persuasive grounds for assuming that a society which acts justly at home will also act justly abroad.

Why do radicals either neglect or dismiss these altogether commonplace considerations? In part, the answer must be found in the view that the world as we know it today is America's special creation. "The elimination of American hegemony," one radical declares, "is the essential precondition for the emergence of a nation and a world in which mass hunger, suppression, and war are no longer the inevitable and continuous characteristics of modern civilization."[49] In this view, it is the hegemony of a Capitalist America that perpetuates mass hunger in India, suppression in the Soviet Union and China, and conflict between Israel and Egypt, India and Pakistan,

[49] Gabriel Kolko, *The Roots of American Foreign Policy*, p. 87.

and China and the Soviet Union. What a hegemonic Capitalist America has created, a truly Socialist America may destroy.

This extreme version of America's all-encompassing power for maintaining the evil that presently exists in the world is not shared by all radical critics. Some acknowledge that the world of a Socialist America, however humane and democratic this socialism, would still be a world of conflict, if only for the reason that it would still be a world divided into sovereign states. They might well argue that a Socialist America would alleviate hunger in India to a degree a Capitalist America is either unwilling or incapable of doing, but they do not insist that a Socialist America would form the essential precondition for resolving the present differences between China and the Soviet Union. (If this conflict holds out dangers to a Capitalist America, there is no apparent reason for believing it would not hold out dangers to a Socialist America. Moreover, if it is once conceded that a Capitalist America is not responsible for the Sino-Soviet conflict, and the aspirations that conflict reveals, it must also be conceded that there is little reason for believing that a Socialist America would moderate either Soviet or Chinese aspirations generally. If anything, we must expect that the kind of America the radicals look forward to would cause Soviet and Chinese behavior to become much less moderate than it is today.)

Even so, there is no essential disagreement among radicals on the manner in which the new society would behave. If this vision is immune to the considerations we have earlier raised, it is because the radical is not concerned with men as they have been but with men as they might and presumably will be once they have been emancipated from the existing social order. It is only a view which assumes the past to be irrelevant in projecting the future that can entertain the expectation of a Socialist America's providing a generous measure of assistance to poor states for no other reason than the desire to alleviate suffering. What a Capitalist society is presently incapable of doing for its own, a Socialist society will do not only for its own but for others as well. The radical belief in the foreign policy of a Socialist America ultimately rests on the assertion—a tautology—that if men are transformed they will then behave differently. If we believe that a "humane and democratic" socialism will lead to the transformation of men, to a new beginning in history, then it indeed follows that America would behave toward the world in the manner radicals confidently expect. But this is to resolve the problem of how a Socialist America would behave by defining the problem away.

IV. A CONCLUDING NOTE

We have had earlier occasion to remark upon the influence exerted by the radical critique. That it has exerted an influence is clear. What is not clear is the extent of this influence, whether on a conventional historiography or on a generation of students. Against the claim of a marked impact on a conventional historiography, it may be argued that a revised interpretation of the origins and subsequent course of the cold war would have occurred in any event. On this view, a greater measure of detachment and objectivity is the result of the passage of time and the cooling of passions. At least a moderate revisionism is thus the expected and even the natural consequence of a more distant perspective. So too, against the claim of a substantial impact on a generation of students, it may be contended that the emergence of a deeply skeptical outlook among the young is only the expected consequence of events the young have directly experienced. Given these events, and the evident distrust and disillusion they have created, to search for other explanations of a transformed outlook toward America's role and interests in the world is merely to push at a door that is already open.

It is not easy to respond to such arguments as these which reject the view that the radical critique has had a significant influence. With the passage of time, and particularly with the passing of the classic cold war, a moderate revisionism within the framework of a still conventional historiography was to be expected. Nor can the primacy of events in effecting a transformation of outlook among the young be denied. Moreover, whereas the impact of events is—or, at least, seems—readily discernible, the impact of a critique—itself largely a response to the same events—is not. In the case of the younger generation, it is not enough to point out that, as evidenced by books read and discussed, radical criticism has enjoyed a considerable vogue. For the question remains whether it is just that, a vogue. Even if it does go beyond the merely fashionable, we may still have no reliable way of knowing how deep an impression radical criticism has made. We all take what we want from books. That students share this characteristic can occasion little surprise.

It these considerations fail to prove that radical criticism has not had a substantial influence, they serve to warn of the hazards in advancing a contrary claim. There are no existing studies that have sought to isolate and to gauge this influence. Nor is there much prospect that such studies could be successfully undertaken, in view of the intrinsic difficulties they would incur. In the absence of more reliable evidence, we are therefore thrown back upon personal observation (and, inevitably, intuition), the value of which in the present context must be distinctly limited. Even so, it scarcely seems excessive to contend that radical criticism has been a significant factor in the emergence of a moderate revisionism, just as it has been a significant factor in the development of an outlook the basic impetus of which has admittedly come from events. Indeed, if all that can be said of the radical critique is that it forced the pace of changes that were already in the making, this is, in itself, an achievement of no small importance.

147

Whatever influence the radical critique may enjoy, its intrinsic merits must be judged quite separately. Despite the treatment radical criticism has generally received at the hands of conventional critics (who have dismissed it even while responding to its more persuasive features), as an interpretation of American diplomacy this criticism does have merit. If nothing else, the radical critique has forced us to acknowledge the extent to which an obsessive self-interest has been central in American foreign policy. In doing so, it has provided an element of realism that, ironically enough, has often been missing from a conventionally critical historiography which has prided itself precisely on its realism. In its insistence that American diplomacy has been driven throughout by self-interest, the lesson radical criticism conveys is that America has behaved very much as other great nations have behaved, and that if there is a quality unique to American diplomacy it consists in the greater than usual disparity between ideals professed and behavior.[1] This lesson may not have been the intention of radical critics—certainly this was not their primary intention—but its corrective value is not diminished for that reason.

It is also the merit of radical criticism to have shown that American diplomacy scarcely betrays the intellectual error attributed to it by a conventionally critical historiography. To the latter, America's glo-

---

[1] Anyone who doubts this need only turn to accounts, which are anything but radical, of America's relationships with Cuba and the Philippines. The disparity between professed ideals and behavior is such that it must startle even the complacent. See, for example, George E. Taylor, *The Philippines and the United States: Problems of Partnership* (1964), and John Plank, ed., *Cuba and the United States: Long-Range Perspectives* (1967).

balism—and interventionism—spring from illusory judgments of the world and particularly from the conviction that America's wants and values are shared by men everywhere. That we persist in this conviction proves to the conventional critic that America is still isolationist in the deeper sense of remaining an "isolated" nation. It is true that the quality of isolation, the sense of political and moral separateness, may manifest itself both in a policy of isolation as well as in a policy of intervention. In either case, however, the root of policy is presumably the same and consists in the inability to recognize and to accept the world for what it is. The radical critic clearly does not deny our inability to accept the world for what it is. To the contrary, this is a central element of his criticism. What he does deny is that this inability, or unwillingness, is explained by intellectual error. Where the conventional critic finds intellectual error or false perceptions, the radical critic finds the will to establish America's hegemony in the world. Here again, the lesson radical criticism conveys is that America has behaved very much as other great nations have behaved and that her messianism has been a means to the end of hegemony. In emphasizing the deliberate and consistent quality of this will, the radical critic no doubt exaggerates. Even in exaggeration, however, the radical emphasis seems nearer the truth than liberal-realist historiography.[2]

---

[2] And much nearer the truth than this writer when he declared: "America is perhaps history's example par excellence of the state that reluctantly, and apologetically, acquired imperial power." *Nation or Empire: The Debate over American Foreign Policy* (1968), p. 153. Certainly, our apologetics were not matched by our reluctance.

Nor does it matter much whether America's expansionism is seen to reflect a will to hegemony or the desire to shape an environment congenial to American institutions and interests. Even if the latter interpretation is taken, the point remains that America has entertained in this century a very expansive concept of security. Although obscuring its deeper roots, radical criticism has nevertheless illuminated this concept of security in a manner conventional historiography has not done. The radical critique has persuasively demonstrated that the manner in which we have defined our security in its greater than physical dimension has been practically indistinguishable from a world stabilized in a pro-American equilibrium. To this extent, there is much to be said for the radical emphasis on the Open Door as the key to American strategy in this century. For the Open Door not only defined the manner in which American leaders viewed the nation's security in its greater than physical dimensions, it also reflected the aspiration to world leadership that was inseparable from this view. The radical critic may interpret the Open Door too narrowly and identify as policy what has often been little more than aspiration. Even in doing so, he provides a needed corrective to conventional criticism.

Despite these considerations, we cannot conclude that such influence as radical criticism has enjoyed may be attributed primarily to its explanatory power. For the merit of the radical critique must still be weighed against defects examined in earlier pages. These defects, and the illusions they must inevitably foster, cannot be redeemed by the provisional realism which makes the radical so effective a critic, not only of American diplomacy but also of the dominant

interpretation of this diplomacy. Whereas the radical critic clearly sees—indeed, too clearly sees—the
calculation and self-interest that have marked American foreign policy, he persistently ignores the deeper
sources of collective self-aggrandizement. Even if it
were true that America's security in this century has
been totally unconditioned by events occurring beyond our frontiers, it would not follow that our expansion must be attributed to forces generated by a
particular socio-economic structure. There may be
few reliable lessons that the study of state relations
reveals. But one is surely that the identification of
the collective self with something greater than the
self is so endemic a trait in the case of great states
that it may be considered to form part of their natural history. The radical attempt to find the roots
of America's expansion primarily in her institutional
forms dismisses this lesson. It necessarily denies that
it is power itself, more than a particular form of
power, which prompts expansion.

Thus radical criticism will not confront the eter-
nal and insoluble problems inordinate power creates,
just as it will not acknowledge that men possessed
of this power are always ready to use it if only in
order to rule over others. In the radical *weltanschauung* there is little, if any, appreciation that dominion is its own reward and that men may sacrifice
material interest in order to rule (or, for that matter, to be emulated). There is also little, if any, appreciation that expansion may be rooted in an insecurity that is not simply self-generated. It is no
doubt true that America's expansion is in large measure the result of an expansive concept of security
and that this concept is, in part, related to the nature of America's institutions. It is not true that

America's security in this century has been unconditioned by events occurring beyond our frontiers and that, in consequence, to the extent our security has been compromised it has been the result of our own persistent expansionism and aggressiveness. The issue of physical security apart, the radical case proceeds from the assumption that whatever threat there has been to American security in its greater than physical dimensions, such threat has followed either from the way we have mistakenly defined our security (that is, as a function of what were supposedly our institutional needs) or from the objective needs of America's institutions. In neither form, however, does this assumption rest upon a persuasive showing that given different institutions a hostile world would have posed no threat to us. The radical critique takes for granted what must instead be plausibly demonstrated.

If the radical critique thus fails to explain the past satisfactorily, it can scarcely be expected to afford a reliable guide to understanding the present. Indeed, in one important respect, the present yields to this critique even less than the past did. Whereas the radical argument of dependence carries some plausibility when applied to the circumstances of a generation ago, it carries almost no plausibility in the circumstances of today. When applied to the America of World War II, it is not implausible to argue that the need for foreign markets was seen as vital to an economy that had only been raised from depression by war. When applied to the America of the late 1960s, in order to explain a policy of counterrevolutionary intervention, the radical argument of dependence appears almost curious in its archaism. Not only has the objective basis for conviction been trans formed, but conviction itself has eroded. Whatever merit the dependency thesis may have had in an earlier period, it has little if any merit today.

More than the explanatory power of radical criticism, it is the moral fervor and idealism of this criticism that must account for its influence. A provisional realism masks an idealism that runs deep in the American grain. The moral absolutism with which, explicitly or implicitly, the radical judges America's relations with the world is distinctive only with respect to the object of judgment—and condemnation. With respect to the standards of judgment employed, radical criticism is characteristically —if exaggeratedly—American. It is not surprising, then, that it is also characteristically American in its expectations of the role a new America is destined to play in the world. The radical does not foreswear the belief in America's providential mission. Instead, he changes the content of that mission and sees its fulfillment in the future. A condemnation of the past and present is accordingly joined to a promise of a future in which a sinful nation may yet redeem itself and, by so doing, serve as an example to the world. Indeed, given America's wealth, it may yet save the world. In the vision—or illusion—of how a Socialist America would behave, the radical entertains expectations of the nation's destiny Americans have always entertained.

Will the influence of radical criticism persist, if only in attenuated form? To those who attribute this influence almost entirely to Vietnam, the answer is clear. With the passing of the war, the influence of the radical critique will also pass. This view is less than persuasive, however, even after the evident relationship between Vietnam and the spread of radical criticism is acknowledged. For young Americans the Vietnam experience has shaped an outlook that, in the absence of intervening events, may be expected to survive the war, an outlook that may also be expected to prove receptive in some measure to radical criticism. There is the further consideration that Vietnam must itself be placed against the decline in the sixties of the classic cold war. This decline could have been expected to give rise to revisionism, including radical revisionism, quite without the war, and the emergence of the radical critique may in fact be traced to the years immediately preceding Vietnam. With the decline of the cold war, forces of change within domestic society that had long been suppressed were bound to become manifest. In becoming manifest, they were bound to compete for the political energies and resources that had heretofore been devoted to foreign policy. The very fact of this competition would have generated a critical outlook toward the nation's foreign policy, particularly to the extent it could be argued plausibly either that America's security no longer required maintaining the global role and interests to which the cold war had led or that America's role and interests abroad could be maintained by less costly and painful methods. (Not infrequently, both arguments have been urged simultaneously, though they are in part contradictory.)

In this broader perspective, Vietnam may be seen to be as much a precipitant as a cause of the disaffection that enabled radical criticism to gain its present influence. Vietnam illuminated and brought to the fore developments that had long been in the making. In showing that many of America's interests and commitments are the result of a concept of security that can no longer satisfactorily account for these same interests and commitments, the war undermined an essential rationale for sustained activism —and interventionism—abroad. In revealing the imperial root of American policy, the war raised doubts —even among the more credulous—about the meaning of America's purpose in the world (and if not the meaning of this purpose, then its continued relevance to a world that appears increasingly resistant to this purpose and less amenable to American power). In demonstrating, as no other event has demonstrated, the domestic costs of military intervention when a consensus on the necessity (or justice) of intervention cannot be obtained, the war marked the emergence of potentially powerful domestic constraints on American foreign policy. In part, these constraints must of course be seen in terms of the particular circumstances attending the conflict in Vietnam. In part, however, they reflect observable trends in mature industrial societies, trends that will, if anything, deepen in the post Vietnam period and that, other things being equal, are likely to make intervention abroad increasingly difficult.

It is not enough to argue, then, that revisionism has been a recurrent phenomenon in American history, that "past exercises in revisionism have failed to stick,"[3] and that, accordingly, the radical revisionists of today will follow the fate of earlier revisionists. Quite apart from its intrinsic merit, the influence of revisionist thought is largely determined by events. The revisionism of the interwar period, insistent in its isolationism, suffered eclipse when

[3] Arthur Schlesinger, Jr., "The Origins of the Cold War," p. 23.

events in the external world appeared sufficiently threatening to American security interests to compel an interventionist policy. Events, as it were, put the revisionism of the thirties to the test and it failed. Within the coming decade, events may do the same for radical criticism, equally insistent—though for quite different reasons—on isolating a Capitalist America. If it is pointless to speculate on the precise form those events might take, it does seem reasonably clear that they would have to appear as a direct challenge to American security by another great power. Nothing less, it would seem, can shake the skepticism of a generation that has not experienced the problem of insecurity. In the absence of such a challenge, however, the influence of radical criticism may be expected to persist.